MARCO POLO

SEY
CHEL
LES

SOMALIA

INDIAN
OCEAN

KENYA

SEYCHELLES
♂ Victoria

TANZANIA

COMOROS

MOSAM-
BIQUE

MAURITIUS

MADAGASCAR

T0150572

www.marco-polo.com

FREE!

THE TOURING APP

shows you the way...
including routes and offline maps!

2

GET MORE OUT OF YOUR MARCO POLO GUIDE

IT'S AS SIMPLE AS THIS

1 go.marco-polo.com/sey

2 download and discover

GO!

WORKS OFFLINE!

SYMBOLS

INSIDER**TIP** Insider Tip

★ Highlight

●●●● Best of ...

🔆 Scenic view

♻ Responsible travel:
for fair trade and ecology
aspects

(*) Telephone numbers that
are not toll-free

PRICE CATEGORIES HOTELS

Expensive over 3,800 rupees

Moderate 2,300–3,800 rupees

Budget under 2,300 rupees

The prices are for two people
in a double room per night including breakfast (no seasonal
supplements)

**PRICE CATEGORIES
RESTAURANTS**

Expensive over 460 rupees

Moderate 310–460 rupees

Budget under 310 rupees

The prices are valid for a meal
with starter, main course and
dessert but exclude drinks

CONTENTS

MAPS IN THE GUIDEBOOK
(124 A1) Page numbers and coordinates refer to the road atlas
(0) Site/address located off the map Coordinates are also given for places that are not marked on the road atlas
(⋔ A–B 2–3) Refers to the removable pullout map

INSIDE FRONT COVER:
The best Highlights

INSIDE BACK COVER:
Street atlas of Victoria (Mahé)

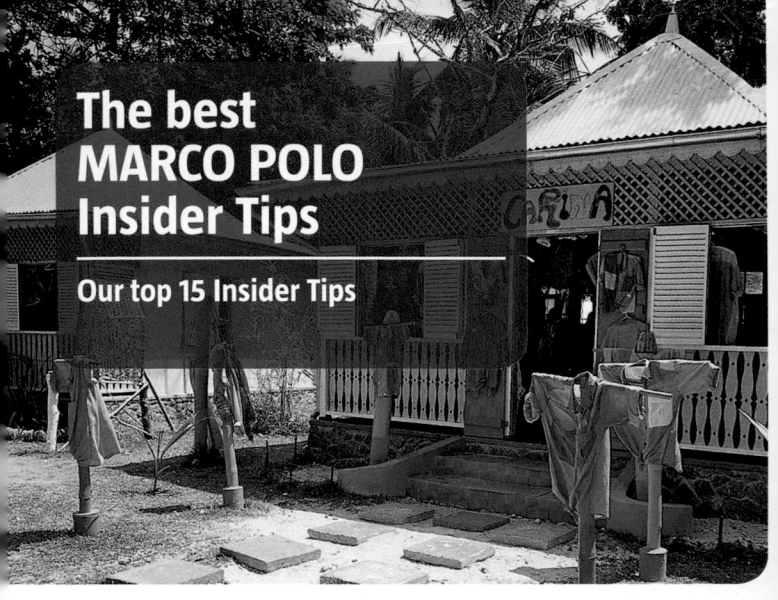

The best MARCO POLO Insider Tips

Our top 15 Insider Tips

INSIDER TIP **Window to the sea**

Enjoy the fantastic underwater world without getting wet: on La Digue the owner of *the Bernique Guesthouse* organises excursions in a glass bottom boat → **p. 58**

INSIDER TIP **Handicrafts made in Seychelles**

In the *Vilaz Artizanal* (craft village) on Mahé, souvenir hunters will find a wide selection of the country's handicraft products on offer. Stroll around the small, neat wooden huts and watch the artisans at work as they make decorative items such as batik and pottery (photo above) → **p. 38**

INSIDER TIP **Cheap and tasty**

At the *Boathouse* on Mahé you can feast until all the dishes are empty: delicious Creole buffet → **p. 34**

INSIDER TIP **Atmosphere and tradition**

Set in verdant tropical gardens with views of the ocean, *Le Méridien Fisherman's Cove* on Mahé has been renovated and is now a discretely luxurious five star resort → **p. 36**

INSIDER TIP **Spices for a king**

Le Jardin du Roi (king's garden) was originally created to compete with the Asian Spice Islands → **p. 37**

INSIDER TIP **Creole delicacies**

At the *Laurier Guesthouse* on the Anse Volbert on Praslin you can enjoy the wonderful Creole buffet and then tumble into bed in your room! → **p. 91**

INSIDER TIP **Life in the coral reef**

Full of colourful fish: the varied marine life in the coral reefs off *Round Island* (photo right) makes for ideal snorkelling conditions → **p. 67**

INSIDER TIP **Happy people on Eden Island**

The harbour on Eden Island is the meeting place every Friday in the *Board Walk* for everyone to share some gossip and enjoy the great music → **p. 48**

BEST OF ...

FOR FREE

● *Market spectacle*

Victoria's vibrant and bustling *Sir Selwyn Selwyn Clarke Market* is open daily from 6am. If you arrive at this time, you can watch as the traders set up their fruit, vegetables, spices and fresh fish and then serve their first customers → p. 45

● *Beautiful jewellery and beautiful paintings*

You can get a good (and free) overview of the artistic work of the many painters and sculptors in the Seychelles at *Kenwyn House* on Francis Rachel Street in Victoria → p. 44

● *Something to snack on*

Sightseeing in the capital Victoria will make you a little peckish. Take a break at one of the small *takeaway restaurants* in the city centre. From about 11am there are Creole dishes at low prices (about 31 rupees) → p. 29

● *The beaches are for everyone*

On the Seychelles there is a law that stipulates that all beaches must be accessible to everyone. This includes the beaches that belong to exclusive hotels, such as the *Banyan Tree* at the Anse Intendance on Mahé. Even if you don't stay there, no one will look at you strangely should you wish to visit the beach (for free) → p. 39

● *A test dive*

The underwater world off the Seychelles is considered to be one of the most beautiful diving sites on earth. If you want to know how you fare with a mask and snorkel, you can do a trial course on Mahé with the *Underwater Centre* at Beau Vallon Bay → p. 38

● *Across the island on a bike*

You can explore the island for just a few rupees when you hire a bicycle from *La Digue Island Lodge*. The bike is the best mode of transport on the island, and bike thieves are virtually unknown because everyone already owns one... (photo) → p. 59

●●●● Dots in guidebook refer to 'Best of...' tips

ONLY ON THE SEYCHELLES
Unique experiences

● *Off to church!*
The Seychellois know how to celebrate and even a *Sunday church* attendance is a celebration – men and women come clad in colourful and festive outfits (photo). A highlight not to be missed: the *procession* for the *Feast of Assumption* on La Digue → p. 108

● *Creole delicacies*
The Creole cuisine is varied and always fresh! One of the most recommended restaurants is *Marie Antoinette* on Mahé, where they have new lunch and dinner menus daily. And because everything is bought fresh at the market, you can be sure that each course on the menu will be a delight! → p. 45

● *A visit to the 'Gauguin of the Seychelles'*
What you also shouldn't miss is a visit to Sir Michael Adams, the Seychelles' most famous painter. His house at Anse aux Poules Bleues on Mahé is surrounded by lush greenery and quite well hidden. If the artist is not available in person, his wife Heather is the right person to speak to → p. 50

● *A coco de mer for the mantelpiece?*
Typical of the Seychelles is the coco de mer, the sea coconut. There is hardly any other fruit on earth that is as steeped in myth as this palm (indigenous to the Seychelles) with its large, heavy nut → p. 20

● *Exploring Aride on foot*
Each Seychelles island has its own botanical and ornithological specialities and this certainly applies to Aride and you can explore the nature reserve on a round trip from Praslin. It is claimed that it has one of the highest densities of lizards in the world → p. 53

● *Giant tortoises*
Once thought to be extinct, their numbers have steadily increased and they are now once again found on many of the islands in the Seychelles. Many of these impressive giant tortoises don't mind being handled, such as Caspar and Caroline on *Cerf Island* → p. 49

ONLY ON

BEST OF ...

RAIN

● *Browse old books*
The history of the Seychelles may not be that old but old books have many stories to tell. That's why it is worth paying the *National Library* in Victoria a visit on a rainy day. The archive includes some special collections and it is very well organised → p. 44

● *Hiking under nature's umbrella*
Hard to believe yet true: a hike through the unique *Vallée de Mai* on Praslin is also an adventure you can undertake in (light) rain. The trees and palms are so dense that the huge leaf fronds serve as the perfect canopy to keep the raindrops at bay. No matter what the weather, sturdy hiking boots are essential → p. 63

● *In the footsteps of the first islanders*
The *National Museum*, in the centre of Victoria on Mahé, is dedicated to the historical heritage of the Seychelles. There you can view some interesting exhibits that include documents about the history of the settlement of the Seychelles, historic nautical charts, models of ships and much more → p. 44

● *Pause for a few minutes*
You don't need to be a Hindu in order to enter the *Arul Mihu Navasakthi Vinayagar* Hindu temple. You can escape a rain shower during a walk through Victoria by spending a few minutes respectfully observing the Hindu ceremonies (photo) → p. 43

● *Dine when it rains*
What can be more romantic than dinner by candlelight with the sound of soft music and the patter of rain outside? One such atmospheric setting is *La Scala* restaurant at North Point on Mahé → p. 34

RELAX AND CHILL OUT
Take it easy and spoil yourself

● *Relax in fragrant herbs*

The spa at the *Four Seasons* hotel on Mahé offers wellness at its finest: their scrubs, wraps and treatments make use of local flowers, herbs and spices based on traditional recipes → **p. 40**

● *Hang out and chill*

The *Pirates Arms*, not far from the Clock Tower in Victoria's city centre, is a popular place so it may take a while for your chilled local ale to arrive at your table but just relax, kick back, see and be seen. The best seating is in the area at the front → **p. 46**

● *Improve your handicap*

There are two golf courses in the Seychelles, one with nine holes on Mahé and one with 18 holes on Praslin (photo). The latter at Anse Kerlan is the nicer of the two, with spectacular views of the Indian Ocean, a treat for the eyes and the senses → **p. 66, 103**

● *The sun salute*

There is one sure cure for sensory overload: yoga! Relax, de-stress, balance the mind and body and find your inner peace with only a few minutes of yoga every day. At the *Maia Luxury Resort* on Mahé you can do so under expert guidance → **p. 41**

● *Relax at reasonable prices*

The spa at the *Black Parrot Suites* in the *Coco de Mer Hotel* on Praslin is brand new and the prices for treatments are quite reasonable. The massage oils are tailor-made to suit the individual – after an analysis of one's karma. Until now, a real insider tip! → **p. 65**

● *Picture-perfect beach*

The perfect beach to day-dream on – it really is truly idyllic – can be found at *Anse Mondon* on Silhouette Island. From La Passe the hike takes just over an hour, but as a reward you can relax and stretch out on the sand and listen to the murmur of the waves → **p. 76**

INTRODUCTION

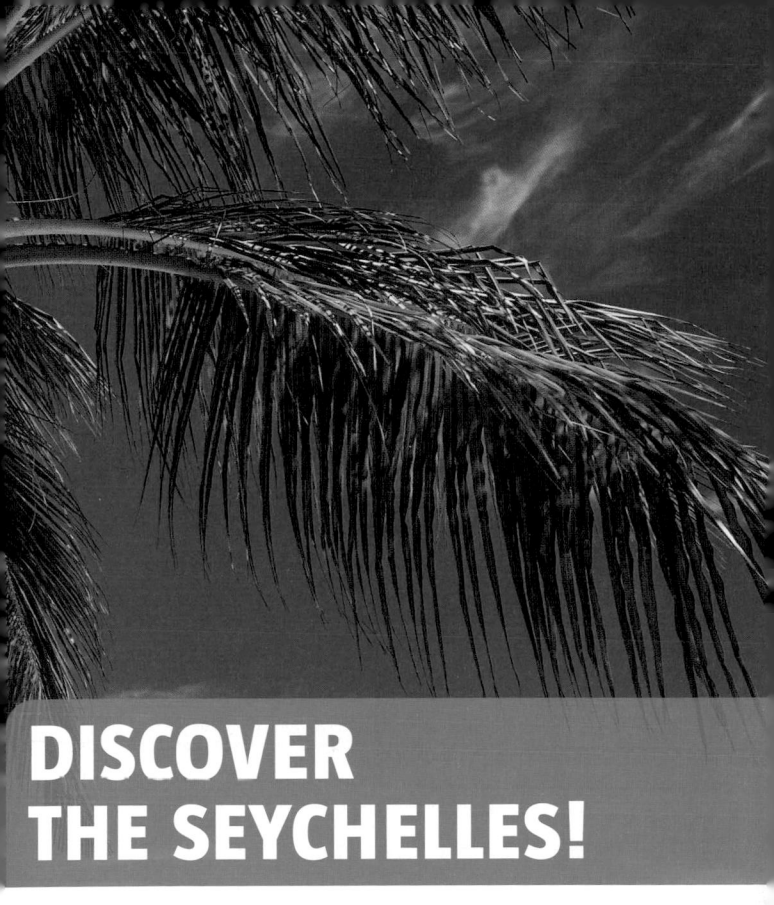

DISCOVER
THE SEYCHELLES!

This much is clear: there is so much more to the Seychelles than its exquisite beaches – it is not just a travel destination for sunbathing and lounging around. The magic of these Indian Ocean islands is multifaceted: the lush tropical vegetation, the exceptional flora and fauna and – last but not least – the friendly, fun-loving people that make a trip to this archipelago off the African coast an *unforgettable experience*.

According to geologists, the largest part of the archipelago is a scattered remnant of the ancient continent of Gondwana. The Seychelles Inner Islands, including the main island of Mahé, consist of granite, which towers up to heights of over 900 m/2,953 ft above sea level and drops off sharply at the coast in bizarrely shaped cliffs and reefs. These rocks are merely the visible tip of a giant underwater mountain range, the Mahé Plateau. Over the course of centuries some *coralline islands and reefs* also formed, making this area famous amongst divers and snorkellers. Stretching far out from the Mahé Plateau is another mighty underwater ridge made of volcanic basalt. This is where the Outer Islands are; a group of coralline islands with fine, white sand. They differ from the granite islands in that

Photo: La Digue

they are very flat with raised coral reefs. If you take all 115 islands together, you would have a surface area of 180 mi². Mahé at 60 mi² is the largest (and most densely populated) island of the Seychelles.

Arab seafarers were the first to set foot on the Seychelles. Around AD 800 they discovered the archipelago on their trade voyages to India. Portuguese seafarers followed suit and in 1502 Vasco da Gama sighted the islands known as the Amirantes, southwest of Mahé. In the 16th/17th century, pirates and buccaneers arrived, most notably the legendary Olivier Levasseur, who called himself 'La Buse' (The Buzzard). He is believed to have buried *a vast treasure*,

before his death by hanging on Mahé, and the booty is still being searched for by treasure hunters to this day. The Seychelles were given their current name in 1756,

Playground for mariners around the world

when the Irish Captain Corneille Nicolas Morphey took possession of the islands under the orders of the French Crown. They were named after Jean Moreau de Sechelles, Louis XV's finance minister. There are plenty of *dazzling personalities* in the history of the Seychelles, such as the Frenchman Quéau de Quinssy, who took over as Governor in 1794. When the British arrived in Victoria with massive superior military forces on 16 May of that year, de Quinssy saw no other option but to sign a capitulation certificate that he had drafted himself. But no sooner had the British ships disappeared over the horizon, than de Quinssy took down the Union Jack and hoisted the Tricolour again. Until 1811 this game was apparently repeated seven times. The annexation of the Seychelles by the British was ultimately unavoidable and in 1833 the new masters abolished slavery. On

Around AD 800
Arab seafarers land in the Seychelles

1502/03
Vasco da Gama discovers the Seychelles en route to India

From 1685
Pirates use the island as a hideout

1756
The Irish Captain Corneille N. Morphey declares Mahé a French colony

1770
French settlers establish the first settlement on Ste Anne

1794–1811
Chevalier Quéau de Quinssy, the island's Com-

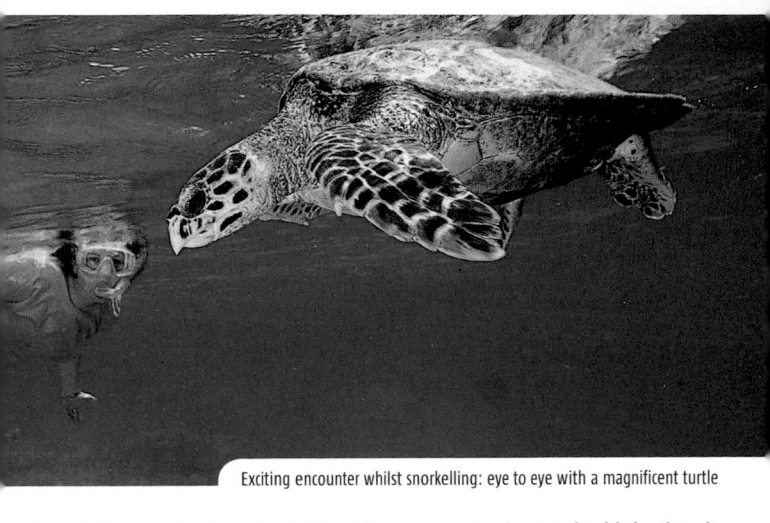

Exciting encounter whilst snorkelling: eye to eye with a magnificent turtle

the outskirts of Victoria on Mahé there is a monument that marks this landmark event. The Zonm Lib is the statue of a man symbolically breaking free of his chains.

Today the Repiblik Sesel (the official Creole name for the Republic of the Seychelles) is regarded as a *relatively stable democracy*, which usually has a socialist-leaning head of state. On the 5th June 1977 the Prime Minister France Albert René took advantage of the democratically elected President James R. Mancham's absence and staged a coup d'etat. From then on René, who studied

Vibrant republic in the Indian Ocean

in Switzerland and England, won all the elections – he effectively ran a one-party state until 1993 – without any opposition to challenge him. But even after 1993, when multiple parties were allowed to participate, René always emerged victorious at the polls. In 2004 he stepped down and handed his office over to his Vice President, James Alix Michel, who was re-elected in 2006 and 2011.

mandant, surrenders eight times to the British, but hoists the French flag repeatedly after their departure

1811
The British annex the islands and prohibit slavery in 1833

From 1875
The Seychelles becomes a place of exile

1903
The British government declares the Seychelles a Crown colony

1964
The Seychelles Democratic Party (SDP) and the Seychelles People's United Party (SPUP) are founded

It would appear that it is of little concern to many Seychellois who heads up the country's parliament. Live and let live is their motto. This attitude is possible because the government provides a social system with free education and primary care in sickness and old age. A further contributing factor is that the standard of living in the Seychelles is considerably higher than in continental Africa. However, the cost of living has risen dramatically in recent years, and many Seychellois now only manage to cope financially by taking on a second job. It is interesting to note that the state provides more than half of the 30,000 jobs in the economy. In 2008,

Fishing, spice trade and tourism

the vast expenditure on social security for the population led to the Seychelles republic being classified as officially bankrupt. The country was only rescued by a 26-million-dollar loan from the International Monetary Fund (IMF). However, certain terms were imposed: more than 1,000 civil service employees were made redundant and the government no longer had control over the exchange rate. Many beaches and land estates were sold to foreign investors. Today, the Seychelles are prosperous again. They are considered to be *the richest Africans* in terms of average per-head income.

The opening of the international airport on Mahé in 1972 heralded the beginning of *organised tourism*, which today represents the main source of income, generating about 70 per cent of state revenue while fishing and fish processing and the spice trade play a less significant role these days. The intention until the turn of the millennium was to cater only to well heeled visitors with luxury accommodation, but with the chronic shortage of foreign currency the current government has decided to promote private initiatives such as guesthouses and holiday apartments. While the Seychelles is still is not a cheap travel destination, an affordable holiday in one of the numerous guesthouses is quite possible. Per year there are only about 220,000 visitors to the islands, the majority of them from Europe.

When you stroll through the Vallée de Mai nature reserve on Praslin, you will be inspired enough to think that God must have had a *creative day* when He scattered these islands off the African coast in the Indian Ocean. None are alike and each has something special to discover. The islands are lush and fertile and if you come

1970
The Seychelles establish their own constitution

1976
The islands gain their independence and James R. Mancham (SDP) becomes the first President

1977
France Albert René ousts Mancham in a coup and is declared the President

1993
René wins the first multi-party elections in 16 years

2004
James A. Michel replaces France Albert René and is re-elected in 2006, 2011 and 2015

Enchanted location: waterfalls in Vallée de Mai National Park on Praslin

from the other side of the equator, you will be impressed by the *myriad of shapes, colours*, scale and the density of the vegetation. But the nature on the islands is not particularly species-rich and not all of it is indigenous anymore. The indigenous forest around the edge of the islands was cleared and – with the exception of a few places – the original vegetation was replaced with new plants. However, you still find plants and animals that occur nowhere else in the world and there are

Giant tortoises and coco de mer

many botanists and ornithologists from all over the world working to preserve the wildlife that is indigenous to the Seychelles and trying to restore the environment. The legendary coco de mer – *the palm nut that has inspired so many myths* – is one of the 80 plants endemic to the Seychelles. Another unique speciality are the giant tortoises, the 'living fossils' of a bygone era. At one point they were near extinction but there are now more than 170,000 specimens on the islands. Also under protection are 13 bird species that only live on the Seychelles, such as the small Brown Noddy, the mighty Frigatebird and the Red-tailed Tropicbird. Like almost all the planet's coral reefs, those of the Seychelles were also affected by the El Niño climate phenomenon. Nevertheless, the country's natural attractions – especially the marine flora and fauna, which has recovered in many places – is still the country's real drawcard and the raison d'être for its tourism trade. As a result the government has placed about half of the total land area and parts of its coastline *under protection* and some of the islands are only open to scientists with tourists only allowed access under exceptional circumstances.

WHAT'S HOT

1 Dear to the heart

Jewellery These souvenirs are both beautiful and long lasting! The creative minds of *Kreolor (Camion Hall | Albert Street | Victoria | Mahé | www.kreolorseychelles.com) (photo)* craft unique necklaces and rings, combs and bangles out of coconut, shells, wood and seeds. The jewellery and craft items reflect old traditions but are also quite modern: pieces made from natural materials, such as metal and stones or colourful fabrics that are ideal for city life.

Island inspiration 2

Art Swaying palms and splashing water – the island is both home to and inspiration for artist George Camille. In his studio *(Kaz Zanana | Revolution Avenue | Victoria | Mahé)* you can watch him while he works. Andrew Gee welcomes visitors to view his works, inspired by the Seychelles, in his studio *(Baie Lazare | Mahé)*, while sculptor, Tom Bowers, *(Santa Maria Estate | Anse à la Mouche | Mahé) (photo)* creates works whose theme are the beauties of the island.

Beautiful fragrances

Island fragrances The Seychelles are a dream for the olfactory senses and the locals have set about capturing their heady scents in little bottles. One such enterprise is *Kreolfleurage (North East Point | Mahé) (photo)*, where they experiment with hibiscus, elephant grass and takamaka resin. You can buy it at *SenP (Camion Hall | Albert Street | Victoria | Mahé)*, at the *Pineapple Studio (Anse aux Poules Bleues)* or on site, where you can also have a guided tour of the facility. At the *Bonjour perfumery (Victoria Estate Building | Victoria, Mahé)* there are no secrets: you can experience the contents of the perfume yourself.

There are lots of new things to discover on the Seychelles. A few of the most interesting are listed below

Jump in

Sporty Diving, sailing, snorkelling – these are the usual activities on the Seychelles but there are also other sports on offer. What only a few people know is that the wind blows off the Seychelles and the perfect surfing and windsurfing months are from June to September. The professionals from *Tropicsurf (www.tropic surf.net)* know where a breeze is currently blowing on the private island Frégate. The company specialises in surf trips that include candlelight dinners on the beach and excellent wines and accommodation. Even if the wind is not blowing, you can still get on to the water: with stand up paddle board surfing you don't need any wind, but you do need a long paddle *(c/o Four Seasons | Petite Anse | Mahé)*. Another option is to explore the dive world a little faster with a sea scooter. This environmentally-friendly machine is an ideal (and fast) way for divers and snorkellers to get from one dive site to the next *(c/o Angel Fish Dive Operations | Roche Caiman | Mahé)*.

From the garden

...to the table The produce on your plate at *La Plaine St André (Mahé)* is absolutely fresh as it is sourced from their own garden, and the ingredients used at *North Island Resorts (Mahé, photo)* are just as fresh, as they too grow their own produce in their garden. *Maria's Rock Café (Baie Lazare | Mahé)* is in an unusual location, tucked away in a cave; they prepare the fish dishes at your table on hot lava stones and serve them with vegetable side dishes. The latter often harvested by Maria Soubana herself such as the local chilli variety the *pimente kabrí*, which flourish in Soubana's mother's garden.

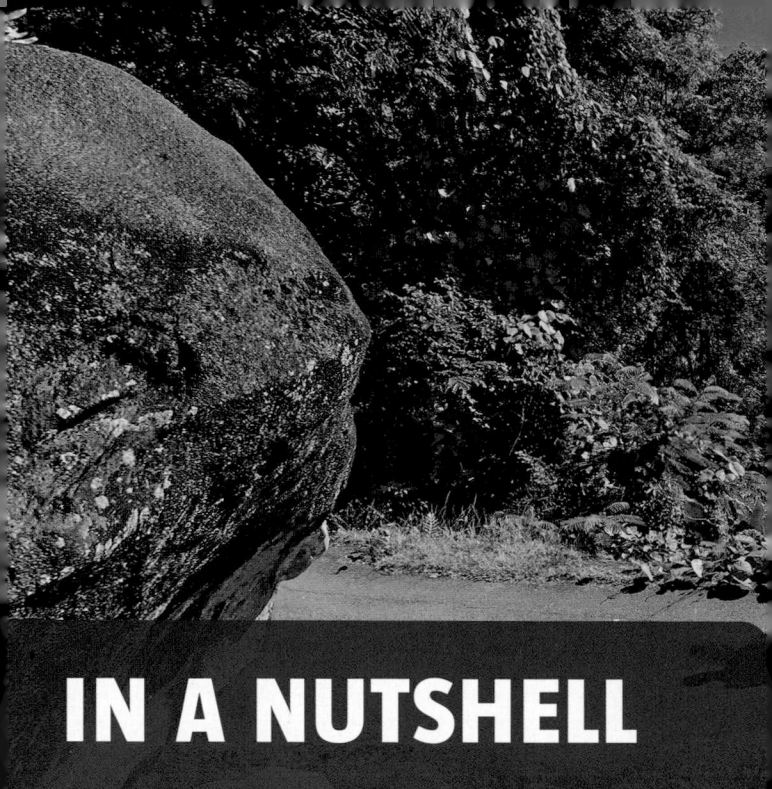

IN A NUTSHELL

POPULATION

About 87,500 Seychellois, in Creole *Seselwa*, live on the 115 or so islands that make up the Republic of the Seychelles. There is no indigenous population and the Seychellois are a diverse ethnic mix of immigrants. The population is concentrated on the two islands of Mahé and Praslin – and a few smaller islands in the surrounding area – where close to 90 per cent of the population lives. The population density is the greatest on Mahé. The Seychelles has a very young population: almost a quarter of the inhabitants are currently under the age of 14 years and the average age is about 28 years.

COCO DE MER

A botanical rarity, the ● *coco de mer*, is unique to the Seychelles and grows only on Praslin and Curieuse (a few specimens are also in the Botanical Gardens in Victoria). The coco de mer got its name even before the discovery of the Seychelles. The nuts were carried on the ocean currents and deposited on distant shores where they were thought to be the fruit of a huge underwater tree. Everything about the coco de mer is large: the seed from which it grows is considered the largest in the botanical world, the trunk makes its way up through even the densest of forests, and the nut itself weighs a good 20 kg/44 lbs. The leaves have a wide surface and their stems are long so that they can compete against other plants for sparse sunlight. The manner in which the coco de mer propa-

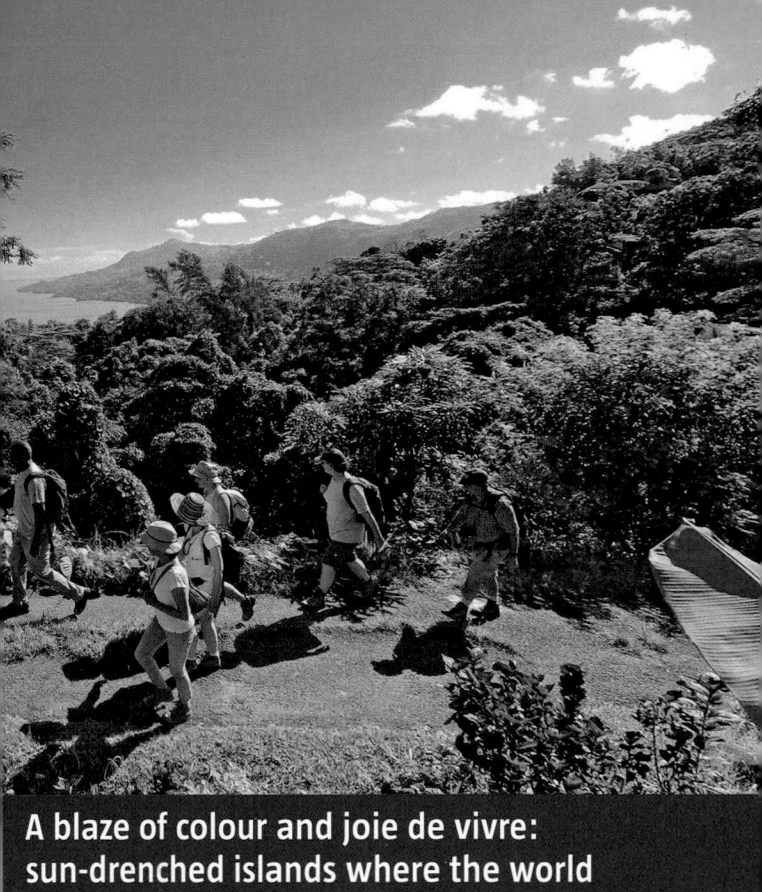

A blaze of colour and joie de vivre:
sun-drenched islands where the world
is still a wonderful place

gates also has a local legend. The male plant has a phallus-like extension, the matching counterpart can be found in the fruit of the female plant. On stormy nights, according to the Seychellois, the male trees uproot themselves and approach the female trees to reproduce, a process that no one has managed to capture yet. While the pollination is still not fully understood, botanists have a far more profane explanation: the ripe nuts fall to the ground, and after about one year a seedling takes roots and over the course of many years it becomes a tree. It takes a quarter of a century for the young tree to bear its first fruit. Its life expectancy is about 200 to 400 years. For centuries the coco de mer nut was considered a symbol of wealth and prosperity. Today it is a popular, if somewhat large souvenir from the Seychelles; about 2,000 are sold to tourists each year.

ESMERALDA & CO.

Nowhere else in the world are there as many giant tortoises as on the Seychelles. The largest and oldest among them is Esmeralda who, despite the name, is actually a male. He weighs in at about 298 kg/657 lbs and is believed to be about 120 to 150 years old. These sedate creatures are relics of a past epoch tortoise meat, specifically tortoise soup. In addition, access to their nesting and breeding sites was also restricted. Since then the number of tortoises has grown significantly and today there are an estimated 170,000 giant tortoises on the

Rare species: White Terns on Bird Island

and were culled to the point of extinction, because when the first seafarers arrived at the Seychelles, these creatures served as a practical source of meat and when the ships set sail again they frequently took dozens of live tortoises on board, which were then slaughtered for fresh meat during the course of the voyage. The result was a drastic depletion of the species. The end to the slaughtering of these animals was first brought about when the government introduced a protection measure and then by the international condemnation of the enjoyment of Seychelles. Most of the animals live on the Aldabra Atoll, and Moyenne Island has one of the world's largest populations with 100 specimens.

FAUNA

On Bird Island you won't only get to know Esmeralda, but also – as with the other islands – many exotic birds such as the *Sooty* and *White Tern*. On La Digue you can see the rare *Paradise Flycatcher*, on the Aldabra Atoll the *White-throated Rail* and the *Aldabra Drongo*, a songbird. There are also countless species of seagulls, swallows and other birds that are typical of the tropics, such as the *White-tailed* and *Red-tailed Tropic-bird*. The *Great Frigatebird* are the most powerful seabirds, with a wingspan of up to 2 m/6.6 ft, while on the island of Frégate there is a zoological rarity, the *Seychelles Magpie Robin*. Destruction of their habitat put them on the brink of extinction only a few years ago but, due to preservation efforts, there are now about 80 specimens of this inconspicuous black and white bird. Some interesting *lizards, salamanders* and *geckos* also reside here. The latter are particularly popular because they like to eat vermin.

FLORA

There was once a time when almost all the islands were covered with dense tropical forest. Today the vegetation is shaped by mankind but this has made little dent in the country's natural splendour. The largest diversity can be found on the main island of Mahé but it is also here where you will find visible traces of man's careless treatment of nature: where mangroves and hardwood forests once stretched out, there are now secondary forests with low species diversity and alien vegetation. They consist mostly of coconut palms and the imported species of *Eucalyptus* and *Albizzia,* as well as ornamental plants such as *hibiscus* and *bougainvillea*. The indigenous forests are now only found in the higher elevations.

In the Seychelles there are many plants that cannot be found – or found only in small numbers – anywhere else in the world. Some of them were not always indigenous; many species were brought in as seeds or seedlings from other islands and some are botanical rarities, such as the *bwa-d-fer* (Ironwood tree), with only a few surviving, or the *Jellyfish*

tree, whose flowers look like an upside down jelly fish. Also only found in the Seychelles is the aromatic *Seychelles Vanilla Orchid* with its large, white flowers. There are countless palm trees, one of which provides *palm of hearts*, a vegetable harvested from the core and tips of the palm and is used to make the exquisite 'Millionaire's Salad'. The country's two most economically important trees are the coconut tree – they are processed from root to palm leaf – and *cinnamon tree,* which was introduced from Ceylon (now Sri Lanka) in 1772 by the French Governor Pierre Poivre. The smooth, aromatic bark of the tree is either ground into a spice or stripped and dried into small, curled sticks. Whilst its cultivation was for many years unprofitable, today it is a thriving industry. Further important spice plants are *clove, vanilla, citronella* and *patchouli.*

GEOGRAPHY

The Seychelles archipelago Economic Exclusive Zone extends over a surface area of more than 385,000 mi² but of that the actual land area is 175 mi². Topographically the Seychelles belong to the African continent; the Inner Islands are the scattered remnants of the geologically ancient super-continent of Gondwana. The Inner Islands with an area of about 12,000 mi² include 32 islands, almost all of which are granite. The Outer Islands area covers about 155,000 mi² and these islands are primarily reef islets and low-lying coral islands such as the Amirante and the Aldabra Atoll. The distance between the main island of Mahé and the African mainland is about 1,600 km/994 mi.

CLIMATE

The Seychelles has a tropical climate with consistent temperatures throughout the year. The average temperature is 26.6 °C/80 °F and it seldom gets hotter than 32 °C/90 °F. The months of May to October are pleasant and dry but there can be strong southeastly monsoon rains. December to March are hotter and more humid and the monsoon comes from the north-west. However, given the large expanse of the archipelago, the climatic conditions do vary depending on the region. The water temperature is stable throughout the year at 26–30 °C/79–86 °F and the sun shines on average for 6–8 hours a day. Mean relative humidity is around 75% with cooling breezes.

CREOLE

Creole developed in the overseas territories of European colonial powers, where the local languages and dialects mixed with the language of the colonizers. The Creole spoken on the Seychelles is *Seselwa* and is based on French phonetics and syntax. Today it is an official language and is used in schools as the official language of instruction.

NATIONAL PARKS

The islands of Aride, Cousin and Curieuse as well as Morne Seychellois National Park on Mahé are all protected national parks and reserves. The Vallée de Mai on Praslin and the Aldabra Atoll are both World Heritage Sites and parts of the ocean surrounding the islands also fall under protected areas. Bathing is allowed in these protected areas on condition that swimmers show respect for nature. The following are two of the most interesting Marine National Parks: *Baie Ternay* at the westernmost tip of Mahé is a narrow bay only accessible by boat. Damaged in the past by divers the coral reef is now slowly regenerating. It has a rich marine life and some diverse

sea grass (e.g. *Turbinia*) and it is the spawning ground for hawksbill turtles. The *Curieuse National Park* is off the coast of Praslin; the reserve covers 3,650 acres of which four-fifths is land and one-fifth water. The park includes the island of Curieuse as well as the channel which separates the island from the Anse Boudin. Some of the island's protected species include hawksbill turtles, giant tortoises, the iconic coco de mers as well as the mangrove forests of Turtle Bay.

POLITICS

One might think that the Seychellois live in paradise: free education until university level, free medical and hospital treatments, a state guaranteed pension and other social services. For the local population these are the positive consequences of a government that ran for decades along Socialist lines. The introduction of these benefits was only possible with the energetic support of other Socialist governments, such as the former Soviet Union and East Germany. This massive development aid made the Seychelles – in comparison to its neighbours on the African continent – a prosperous welfare state that was soon able to realize dreams that were nearly impossible in other countries.

With the demise of the Soviet Union and the dissolution of East Germany came the end of the aid subsidies, and any increase in the revenue from tourism could hardly offset the loss of income. The result was a new policy, in which the former head of government France Albert René was forced to agree to privatisation, which diminished the government control of the economy. But this brought only partial success and in the mid 1990s the Seychelles experienced an acute shortage of foreign currency. René's successor, James Alix Michel, facilitated foreign business ventures and set up a free port, which made the Seychelles into a hub for the trade in goods. And lastly, the government granted permission for the construction of new hotels and guest accommodation which could also be run by private individuals in the form of guesthouses. It is now also the government's declared aim to encourage the tourism sector to become more environmentally friendly and to practice sustainable tourism through conservation.

RELIGION

Almost 90 per cent of the population are Catholic and going to mass on Sundays plays a major role in the lives of most Seychellois. However, many Seychellois secretly maintain their beliefs in superstitions, mysticism and witchcraft – similar to the West African voodoo cults – a syncretism that is typical for former slave areas. The seers or *bonom di bwa* are called upon when, for example, someone wants to find out why a partner is behaving strangely, or why someone has died a sudden death.

ECONOMY

The most important sector of the economy is tourism, which brings in over 70 per cent of the foreign exchange revenue and about a third of the gross national product. Other significant contributors are fishing and the production of copra, the main export product until a few decades ago. Dried coconut is used as a raw material in the chemical industry and is used in the production of soap, shampoo, detergent, candles and synthetic resin varnish. The coconut plantations occupy most of the utilised agricultural area and provide the major-

A chat in Creole

ity of the population with work. Industry exists only on a modest scale, but the government is seeking new sites on Mahé for the establishment of manufacturing companies. The most important export commodities include frozen and canned fish, copra and spices such as cinnamon and vanilla.

FOOD & DRINK

The term 'Creole cuisine' is strictly speaking not precise enough for that which is boiled, grilled and baked in Seychellois pots, pans and ovens. It is far better speak of it as 'Seychelles cuisine', one that – inspired by the ethnic diversity of the locals – is a blend of various other national cuisines.

Each demographic group has contributed different *elements from their own cooking* so there are Asian, Indian and African as well as European dishes that form part of the local cuisine. The latter are the remnants of the colonial era. The Seychellois rarely season with strong spices, more often than not they make use of a combination of fragrant spices such as turmeric, cloves, cinnamon, ginger, garlic, mint, pepper, cardamom and nutmeg. The *careful combination* determines whether or not the dish's main ingredient has a taste of its own and is not overpowered by spices. Another strong influence from Indian cuisine are the *curries*, of which there are a wide variety of dishes, each one of them distinguished by its own individual flavour. Popular favourites are vegetable curries, where different types of vegetables are cut into small pieces, cooked in a pot and seasoned with the aforementioned blend of curry spices. Delicious fish (such as Bonito) curries are also often on the menu and if a curry is too hot, it is softened with coconut milk.

The *main courses* are generally fish, chicken or beef. Fish is cheap; it is

The Seychelles cuisine is fresh, down to earth and characterised by rice and fish dishes, but it also offers some delicious surprises

caught all around the islands and usually sold on the same day. But there are also some differences and certain fish, such as Bonito (part of the tuna family) are considered a poor man's fish. Others are more expensive (and therefore *holiday treats* for the locals) such as swordfish, octopus and mackerel, which you can find on almost every restaurant menu. A typical Seychelles speciality is *bourzwa* or Red Snapper. It is usually served whole and due to its size is enough for the whole table. The swordfish is also delicious and is usually served as a thick, grilled steak. Some of the special delicacies are *lobster, crab and crayfish*, they are usually served grilled.

A meal often begins with a soup (called *bouyon* regardless of the ingredients). Among the starters the *Millionaire's Salad* comes out tops, deserving of its name. The salad is made with heart of palms, in order to get to the edible heart of the palm you need to cut down the whole palm. As this is prohibited,

LOCAL SPECIALITIES

bouyon bred – cabbage soup seasoned with various spices such as garlic, ginger and pepper

kari pwason – a variety of different fish are used to make this fish curry, which has a slightly sour taste from the tamarinds

kari zourit – creamy octopus curry, which is prepared with fresh coconut milk and cinnamon leaves

ladob banann – popular dessert of bananas cooked with sugar, salt and vanilla in coconut milk

lasos kreol – Creole sauce made from tomatoes, onions, bilimbi fruit, garlic, ginger and chilli and used as a fish marinade or sauce

lasoup pwason – soup made of tender, white fish fried with onion in oil and then simmered with spices

lasoup tektek – mussel soup made from tiny white mussels that are collected on the beach, often prepared with pumpkin

pwason griye – grilled fish (e.g. tuna) that has first been marinated in garlic, ginger, onions and peppers and is then served with rice and a spicy Creole sauce

pwason sale – salted, dried (and therefore preserved) fish that is usually offered during the seasons when the fish are scarce (during the south-east monsoons)

satini – all dishes go well with these spicy chutneys made of local fruits such as mango, papaya and coconuts

stek ton – fresh tuna fish, first marinated in Creole sauce and then grilled or baked

they have to wait until a palm falls by itself and since this rarely happens – much to the chagrin of gourmets – the price is very high. In restaurants rice is served with every meal, sometimes also potatoes, mostly in the form of fried chips. The locals prefer manioc, sweet potatoes, breadfruit or green bananas as a side dish.

An expensive dessert delicacy is the very sweet jelly-like *flesh of the green coco de mer*. For the average citizen there are also affordable fruits cooked in a sweet coconut milk sauce called *daubes*. And of course there are bananas – the smaller they are, the sweeter they taste. Passion fruit, avocado, papaya and oranges are offered fresh at

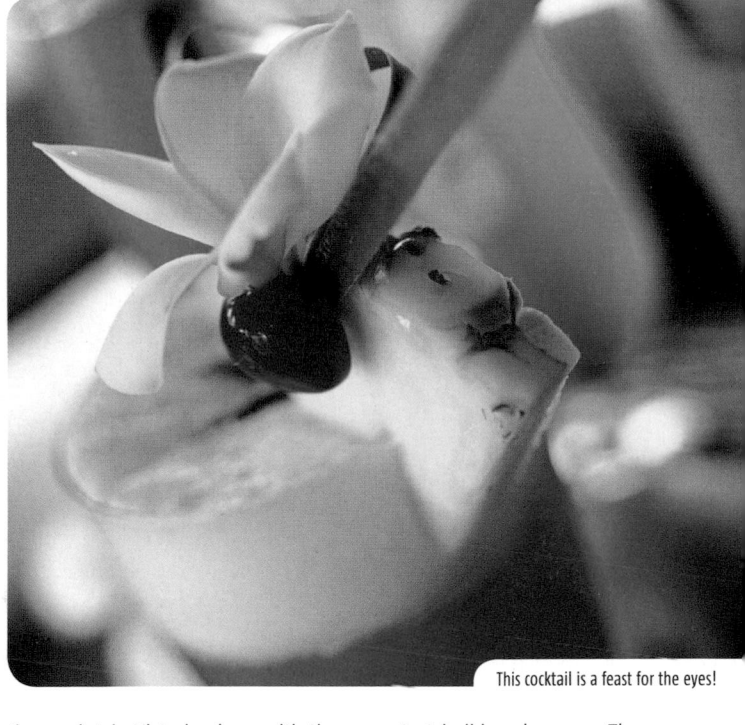

This cocktail is a feast for the eyes!

the market in Victoria along with the all important coconut, which provides not only a refreshing sap but also some delicious white flesh.

Also among the drinks on the islands is a local speciality, the *calou*. This is the half-fermented sap of unripe coconuts, which has a slightly intoxicating effect. Although there are alcoholic drinks, they are imported which makes them quite expensive. One exception is the *Seybrew* beer, which is brewed near Victoria, according to German purity standards.

Each hotel in the Seychelles operates at least one restaurant, but non-guests are welcome almost everywhere. But if you only dine in the hotel restaurants you will be missing out on one of the greatest holiday pleasures. There are a whole range of speciality restaurants on Mahé, Praslin and La Digue, which serve the most *delectable Creole dishes*. Recommended restaurants are found in the main chapters of this travel guide in the 'Food & Drink' section.

In the Seychelles you will search in vain if you are looking for McDonald's or any other fast food chains, this (supposed) gap is filled by several small ● *take-away restaurants*, mainly in the capital Victoria. There is very good Creole fare to take away, for example every day from 11 o'clock you can get delicious *samous-sas,* pastries fried filled with spicy vegetables, meat and chicken. One portion is enough for two and only costs about 31 rupees including the plastic spoon.

SHOPPING

Most of the souvenirs shops are in the centre of Victoria, the capital of the Seychelles, where there are a number of small wooden huts displaying local arts and crafts. It is also worth taking a closer look at the items as many of the goods are not from the Seychelles; look out for 'Made in China' tags. Eden Island Plaza shopping mall with more than 50 shops and restaurants is slightly outside the city centre. *(Daily 9am–5pm)*. In Victoria, new buildings are constantly springing up, while Palm Street is an upcoming area where one new shop comes after the next. The small shops in *Trinity House* (Albert Street) are also recommended where you can take a short break at the *News Café*. You will also find several small shops at *Ocean Gate House*, although offers tend to change fairly often.

As usual, classic shopping in Victoria is always a journey of adventure! You will hardly find any designer merchandise: this is wrong place to hunt for international luxury labels. It's best to go with the flow and browse the small shops, for example those on Market Street or glimpse inside one of the unattractive looking buildings like the *Sham Peng Tong Plaza*.

ARTS & CRAFTS

A wide choice of pottery, both artistic as well as plain, on the one hand and batik work on the other hand can be found in the handicraft village *Vilaz Artizanal*, which is located on the road between Victoria and Anse Royale, 14 km/8.7 mi outside from Victoria. Local artisans display their products in small huts *(see p. 38)*. At *Kenwyn House (see p. 44)* on Francis Rachel Street in Victoria there are not only handicraft souvenirs in supply, but also fine jewellery.

COCO DE MER

Probably the heaviest souvenir that you can bring from the Seychelles is the *coco de mer* (known locally as *koko dmer)*. On average 2,000 of these nuts are annually processed into souvenirs; only those with an official certificate may be exported as the palm trees are a protected species. You should expect to pay a very hefty price from 2,300 to 4,600 rupees.

A word of warning: if you try to export a coco de mer without a certificate, you will be issued with a fine, not only when leaving the Seychelles, but also

Model boats and coconuts: only a few souvenirs originate in the Seychelles, but despite this there are plenty of novel gifts

when entering Europe and the coco de mer will also be confiscated.

MODEL BOATS

A souvenir that is not entirely cheap is a true to scale model boat. It is cheaper to buy them at the workshops (rather than in the souvenir shops) and you also get to see just how time-consuming it is to produce a model, such as the 'Santa Maria' from Christopher Columbus' fleet. The model builders from *La Marine Model Ships* in La Plaine St André on Mahé *(Mon–Fri 9am–4pm)* are famed for their craft. A good place to go is also the *Souverains des Mers* boutique in Le Rocher *(5 km/3.1 mi south of Victoria)* with a permanent choice of about 40 models.

STAMPS

The colourful, sometimes large-sized Seychelles postage stamps are careful-ly crafted with exotic, detailed designs that make them a firm favourite with collectors from all over the world and represent at the same time an important source of income for the local post office. The first day covers – as well as individual stamps and complete sets – are highly prized and can be bought at the issue price at a special counter at the main post office in Victoria.

TEA & SPICES

Vanilla, cinnamon and other spices directly from the Seychelles are the most inexpensive at the market in Victoria *(see p. 45)* but they are also available in grocery stores on the other islands. You can also purchase Seychelles tea there, but the choice is somewhat limited.

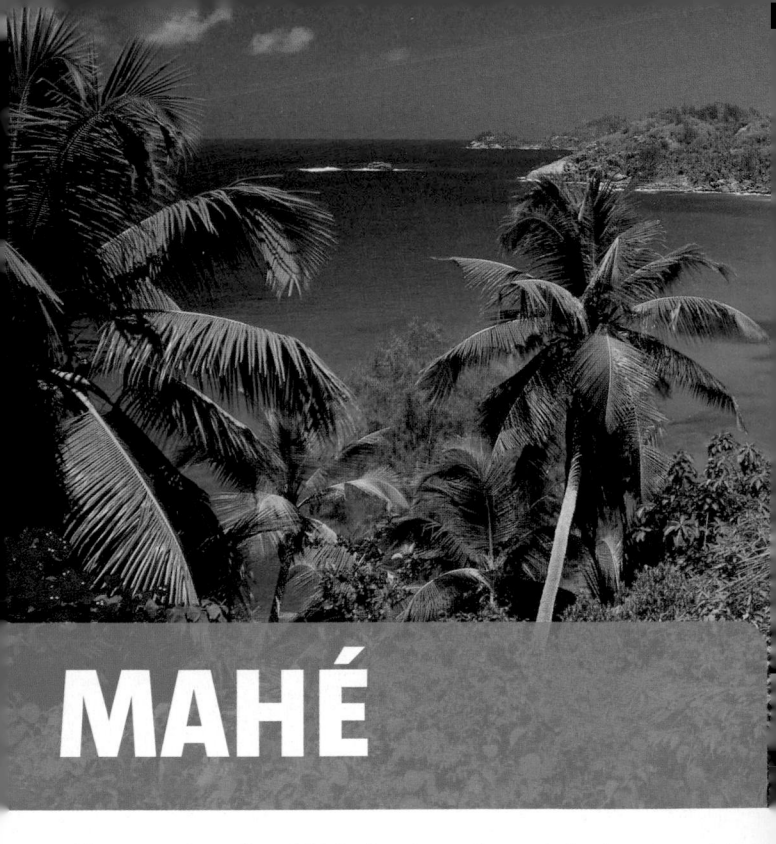

MAHÉ

With an area of 60 mi², Mahé is by far the largest island in the Seychelles – and also the most densely populated. Its length in the north-south direction is 27 km/16.8 mi, its widest point is only 8 km/5 mi. Mahé is usually the first point of contact for all visitors, because the only international airport is located here.

Like most of the islands in the Seychelles, Mahé is also a granite island. Its highest summit ☀ *Morne Seychellois* is situated south of Victoria and reaches 905 m/2,969 ft. Other outstanding topographic features are the summits of *Trois Frères* (699 m/2,293 ft), *Morne Blanc* (667 m/2,188 ft) and *Mount Harrison* (688 m/2,257 ft). These lofty peaks are often covered in thick mist. The west

is more fragmented and more mountainous than the flatter east. The most beautiful beaches on Mahé can be found on the west coast: *Grand' Anse,* the *Anse à la Mouche* and the *Baie Lazare.* Between the capital Victoria and the international airport an entire coral lagoon was drained out for the 1993 Indian Ocean Games. Modern sports venues and housing developments were built on the site. Since the interior of the island is difficult to build on, land on the east coast was reclaimed with landfills in the years before the turn of the millennium. Now known as *Eden Island*, it was developed as an exclusive residential marina by a South African investor and there are now 450 luxury houses and apartments for wealthy Seychellois and foreigners. The

Palm trees, beguiling beaches and a peaceful capital: when you arrive, you might find your own little paradise on earth right here

artificial island with lagoons and piers is connected to the mainland by a causeway *(www.edenisland.sc)*.

NORTH POINT/BEAU VALLON

North Point (124 A1) *(𝄞 D7)* is situated at the end of the route heading from **Victoria over beautiful Vallon Bay on the west coast to the island's northern tip (124 A1) *(𝄞 D7)*.**

After a few miles heading south you reach Beau Vallon (124 A4–5) *(𝄞 C–D 9–10)* and now you are in the area of Mahé with the most tourist facilities: here you will find a formidable selection of accommodation to choose from, such as the *Coral Strand Hotel* or the nearby *Le Méridien Fisherman's Cove*, with a beautiful stretch of pristine beach. The hotels also take full responsibility for the entertainment of their guests and organise evenings with folklore and music performances, often in conjunction with a Creole barbecue. This is not the place for discos, cinemas or nightclubs though.

It is worth driving a bit further from here,

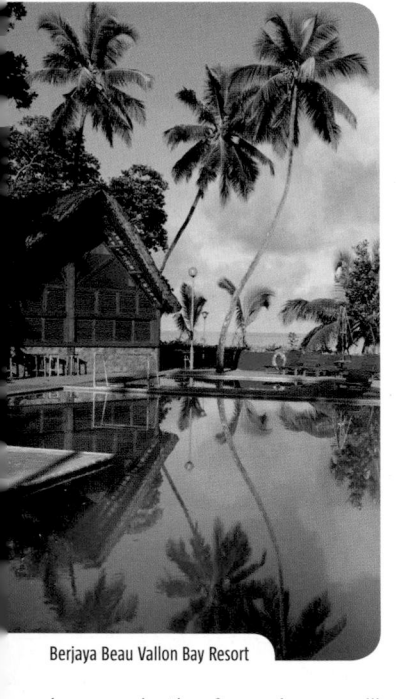

Berjaya Beau Vallon Bay Resort

because shortly afterwards you will come across the place where the legendary pirate La Buse is said to have hidden a huge treasure shortly before his execution in 1730. Treasure hunters are still searching for it to this day. There is no public access to the gravesite but if you walk along the beach you will discover an **INSIDER TIP** intricate system of canals and ditches. It is believed that La Buse hid his treasure in such a way that it would only be found at a specific water level.

FOOD & DRINK

INSIDER TIP BOATHOUSE

It is down to earth and multicultural here and you won't find a menu anywhere. The daily dishes are written up on a chalkboard. For lunch (noon–3pm) there is a set menu, a catch of the day and various curries. In the evenings a Creole buffet dinner is served from 7.30pm. You can keep going back until all the serving dishes are empty which is usually around 10pm. Daily *Beau Vallon Bay | tel. 424 78 98 | www.boathouse. sc | Budget*

LA PERLE NOIRE

Sometimes the chef outdoes himself, at other times it is 'merely' an average Creole meal that comes out of the kitchen. Presumably it depends on the mood of the kitchen staff. There are also Italian and international dishes on the menu. Reserve in advance. *Mon–Sat 7pm–10pm | Beau Vallon | tel. 462 02 20 | Moderate*

LA SCALA ★ ●

One of the best restaurants on Mahé in a magnificent position on a rock at the southwestern end of Beau Vallon Bay. The Italian chef serves classic dishes including home-made pasta and fresh seafood. Expensive, but also very good! *Mon–Sat 7.15pm–9.30pm | Bel Ombre | tel. 424 75 35 | www.lascala.sc | Moderate–Expensive*

SHOPPING

The biggest and best shopping centre, the Eden Island Plaza, is situated slightly outside the city centre (daily 9am–5pm) and has over 50 shops and restaurants. In Victoria, *Palm Street* is an upcoming area where the new shops line up next to each other. Also recommended are the small shops in *Trinity House* (Albert Street) where you stop for a coffee break in the *News Café*.

LEISURE & SPORTS

At *Beau Vallon Bay* you can also find the greatest variety of sports on offer in the Seychelles: waterskiing, windsurfing and parasailing. Fishing and dive trips and sailing boat rentals are all offered by numerous private companies as well as the large hotels.

WHERE TO STAY

BEAU VALLON BUNGALOWS
The small complex only has twelve – very pretty – rooms. The restaurant is famous for its delicious Creole dishes and the owner also organises deep sea fishing trips and excursions to Silhouette Island. *Beau Vallon | tel. 424 73 82 | www. beauvallonbungalows.com | Budget*

BERJAYA BEAU VALLON BAY RESORT & CASINO
An upmarket complex that is still a good value for money. At the beautiful beach various water sport activities are offered. Creole and international cuisine is available in the restaurants. Casino, spa, sports and tennis courts. *232 rooms | Beau Vallon | tel. 428 72 87 | www.berjayahotel.com/mahe | Moderate–Expensive*

COCO D'OR
This friendly guesthouse is set in the midst of a grove of palm trees and practically right on the beach, with 27 air-conditioned rooms and friendly staff. *Beau Vallon | tel. 424 73 31 | www.cocodor.sc | Moderate*

CORAL STRAND
Completely renovated and reopened in 2011/12 this hotel is right on a lovely, long stretch of beach. It has beautiful rooms, is in a quiet location and has a nice piano bar. On the roof is the only

public observatory in the Seychelles, which was previously operated in collaboration with the Laupheim National Observatory *(information at hotel reception). 140 rooms | Beau Vallon | tel. 462 10 00 | www.coralstrand.com | Moderate*

INSIDER TIP HANNEMAN HOLIDAY RESIDENCE

Just a short walk from Beau Vallon Bay lies this very well maintained, new guesthouse with seven large apartments and a lush garden with swimming pool. The owners are happy to organise everything you need for your holiday in the Seychelles, including your rental car. There are shopping facilities for self catering as well as some restaurants nearby. There are also a number of local sporting activities in the area such as diving. *7 rooms | Nouvelle Vallée, Beau Vallon Bay | tel. 442 50 00 | www.hannemanholidayresidence.com | Moderate*

HILTON SEYCHELLES NORTHOLME RESORT & SPA ⚲

With brilliant views of the sea and one of the most beautiful beaches on Mahé, this Seychelles branch of the prestigious hotel chain is naturally rather pricey. If paying about 4,600 rupees per night for one of the completely private luxury villas is not too much for you, then you may be inspired just like Ian Fleming was: he got his idea for the James Bond movie 'For Your Eyes Only' here. The vodka martini cocktail 'shaken, not stirred!' is of course also available at the bar... *39 rooms | tel. 429 90 00 | www.seychelles.hilton.com | Expensive*

INSIDER TIP LE MÉRIDIEN FISHERMAN'S COVE

This thatch and stone five star hotel with all creature comforts was completely renovated in 2004; the ⚲ rooms (all with sea views) are located either in the two storey main building or as chalets, set in lush gardens. *68 rooms | Bel Ombre | tel. 467 70 00 | www.lemeridienfishmanscove.com | Expensive*

LE SANS SOUCI GUESTHOUSE

If you don't place a lot of value on being close to the beach and feel more at home in subtropical nature, you will enjoy this small guesthouse with only four pretty, spacious cottages. Nevertheless, the Beau Vallon Bay is still nearby, and it is only a ten minute drive by car or taxi to Victoria. There is a swimming pool and a ⚲ restaurant that is well known for their Creole cuisine with magnificent views over Victoria and the neighbouring islands. *On the road from Victoria to Sans Souci | tel. 422 53 55 | sansouci@ seychelles.net | Moderate*

SEYCHELLES YARRABEE

Small, family run, self catering guesthouse in Glacis with a spectacular hillside location. The house with three double rooms is particularly well suited for families with children. Beaches for bathing as well as shopping facilities can be found nearby at Beau Vallon Bay; the owners also provide car rentals and lots of insightful travel advice. *Glacis | tel. 426 12 48 | www.seychelles-yarrabee.com | Budget–Moderate*

SOUTH MAHÉ

With regard to the economy and tourism Mahé is geographically extremely 'top heavy' – the southern part of the island is still a true oasis of tranquillity in comparison to the north.

If you don't manage to visit another island during your holiday, you should at

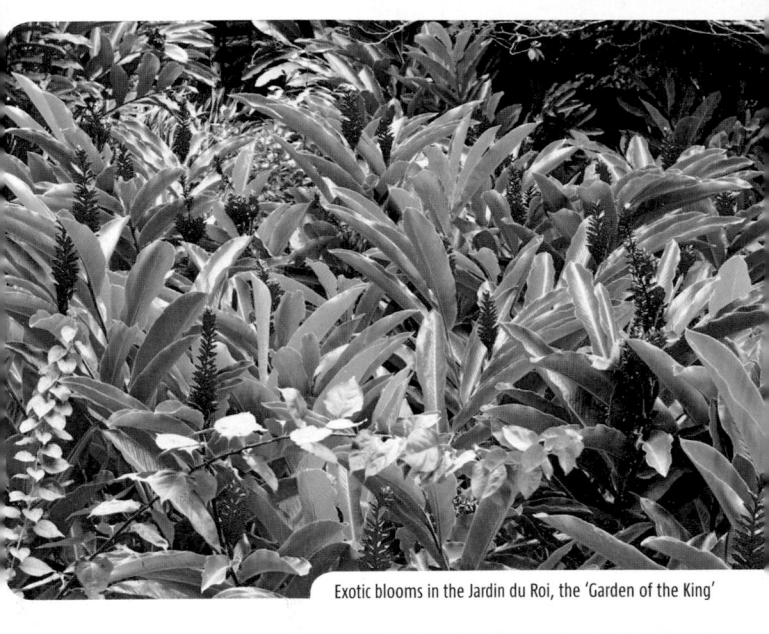

Exotic blooms in the Jardin du Roi, the 'Garden of the King'

least explore the superb beaches and lush interior of south Mahé once.

SIGHTSEEING

ANSE INTENDANCE ★
(130 C5) (*Ø G17*)
Right down in the south of Mahé lies Anse Intendance, possibly one of the most beautiful bays in the world. The long, wide beach is surrounded by impressive granite rocks and the sparkling water is crystal clear, making it ideal for swimming (from October to May). During the other months, there can be a heavy swell with waves breaking on the shore and swimming can be a rather perilous undertaking. You should definitely take heed of any warning signs and tips from the locals in this regard! A visit to Anse Intendance is better suited during the week because at weekends there are many visitors. Above Anse Intendance is

the luxurious five star *Banyan Tree Resort*, with 47 sumptuous private villas and all amenities.

INSIDER TIP ▶ JARDIN DU ROI
(131 D2) (*Ø G16*)
Of the numerous attractions on offer in the Seychelles, the Jardin du Roi (king's garden) is a small gem. Four well sign-posted trails lead through the land-scaped private spice plantation. A hike gives you first-hand impressions of the spice trade of the archipelago. The small crêperie, which is part of the garden, serves delicious pancakes and ice cream. *Near Anse Royale | daily 10am–5.30pm | entrance fee 92 rupees*

LA MARINE
(129 E–F6) (*Ø H14*)
Model building enthusiasts will especially enjoy the faithfully recreated model frigates, schooners and warships made here.

There are certainly cheaper souvenirs on offer in the Seychelles, but definitely not ones so lovingly made. An 18th century era model schooner will set you back about 15,400 rupees. At the arts and craft village, *Vilaz Artizanal (see below)* there is a branch with a workshop. *La Plaine St André | tel. 4375152 | Mon–Fri 7.30am–5pm, Sat 8am–5pm, Sun 9am–5pm*

LOW BUDGET

Set in pretty surroundings, Les Manguiers guesthouse only has three rooms, about 15 minutes by car from Victoria. 1,100 rupees per night per room, self-catering, kitchen available. No air-conditioning! *Machabée | Mahé | tel. 4241455*

Every Wednesday from 5pm there is a small bazaar at the *Coral Strand Hotel*, where you can experience not only local art and music by candlelight, but where you can also buy some pretty and affordably priced souvenirs.

Longing for Italian cuisine? Then you should head to the *Baobab Pizzeria* at the end of Beau Vallon Beach. The wood oven pizzas start from 39 rupees, the restaurant is situated right on the beach. *Daily 11am–11pm | tel. 4247167*

Under no circumstances should you miss out the underwater world of the Seychelles and ● *the Underwater Centre* offers reasonably priced trial diving courses. *Tel 4345445 | www.diveseychelles.com*

POLICE BAY
(131 E6) (∅ H18)

From Anse Intendance it is only a mile or so to Police Bay, yet another spectacular bay. Here the air is heavy with sea spray from the massive waves that crash on to the beach. The currents make swimming impossible and the danger signs should be taken seriously: some swimmers have paid with their lives for their daring. *On the southern tip of Mahé*

INSIDER TIP ▶ VILAZ ARTIZANAL
(129 E6) (∅ H14)

The arts and crafts village, *Vilaz Artizanal,* was created by an initiative of Seychellois artists who decided to market their products collectively. They found a suitable plot of land at Anse aux Pins, against the scenic backdrop of a restored colonial house and in close proximity to the *Vye Marmit* restaurant they built small, neat wooden houses for their products. Besides decorative items (such as batik and pottery) there are also the usual souvenirs on offer. *Domaine de Val des Prés | Au Cap | tel. 4376100 | Mon–Sat 9.30am–5pm*

FOOD & DRINK/ WHERE TO STAY

AVANI SEYCHELLES BARBARONS RESORT & SPA ☆
(128 A4) (∅ E13)

The former *Le Méridien Barbarons* was taken over by the famous Avani hotel chain and after major refurbishment this hotel features again as one of Mahé's top addresses. There are still 124 rooms and suites, some of them with direct access to the wide sandy beach. For a gourmet experience try the *Tamarind* restaurant, while light meals are served in the coffee shop *Elements*. There are also two bars. The spa has an excellent reputation

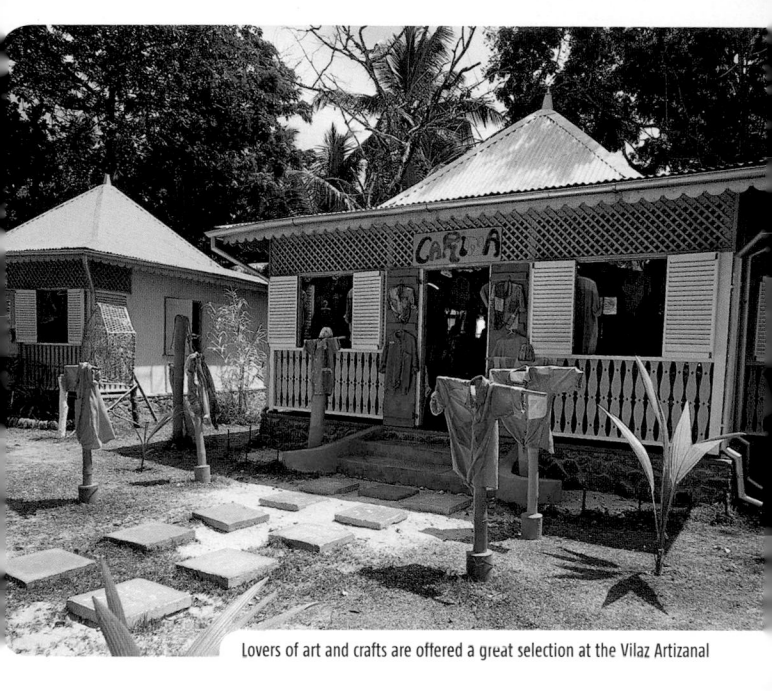

Lovers of art and crafts are offered a great selection at the Vilaz Artizanal

for its wide range of wellness offers. It's an ideal starting point for hiking. *Barbarons | tel. 467 30 00 | www.avanihotels. com | Moderate–Expensive*

BANYAN TREE RESORT ⚕ ●
(130 C5) (*⌖ G17*)
This luxury resort, opened in 2001, was the first step in the government's programme to upgrade establishments on the island of Mahé, whose hotel standards had slipped in comparison to the other islands in the archipelago. Built by a Southeast Asian hotel group, the *Banyan Tree Seychelles*, with its 47 villas – each with private swimming pool – has little to fear from its competitors. To protect the environment the original, rather extensive plans of the investor were scaled back, but despite this the previously undeveloped Anse Intendance –

one of the most beautiful bays in Mahé – has somehow lost its innocence through the building of the hotel. Having said this, a lot of care and attention is being given to environmental protection and sustainable tourism: electricity is largely generated with solar panels and they also have their own waste disposal. The hotel itself – for those who can afford it – will certainly fulfil nearly all your wishes which is why the guests are also understanding when it comes to the fact that they need to travel an hour by car or taxi to get to Victoria. *Anse Intendance | www. banyantree.com | Expensive*

CASUARINA BEACH HOTEL
(129 E5) (*⌖ H13–14*)
This small hotel with only 20 rooms is right on the broad, curving Anse aux Pins beach that is lined with tall palm

trees. Very good value for money. *Anse aux Pins | tel. 4376211 | casuarina@sey chelles.net | Budget–Moderate*

LA GRANDE MAISON (129 F6) *(⌖ H14)*
The restaurant is in an old colonial plantation house amidst the unspoilt planta-

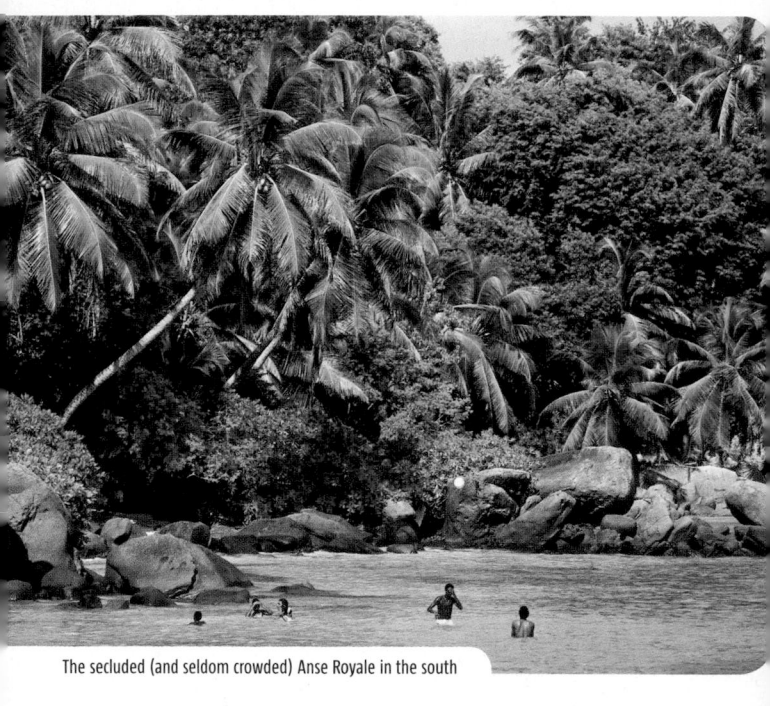

The secluded (and seldom crowded) Anse Royale in the south

FOUR SEASONS RESORT SEYCHELLES
⛱ (130 A3) *(⌖ E16)*

A beautiful, world-class hotel and if you value refined luxury, you will feel right at home here. The resort's 67 private villas, each with their own small swimming pool, are situated on a slope so they all have unrivalled views over Petite Anse and the islands. There are two restaurants, serving Creole and international cuisine, a bar and a ● spa, where the therapies on offer include those made with local herbs and spices. *67 rooms | Petite Anse, Baie Lazare | tel. 439 30 00 | www.fourseasons.com/ seychelles | Expensive*

tion of Plaine St André. Here, fine Takamaka rum is still distilled the traditional way and you can enjoy fine dining tropical style: Creole ingredients combined in exciting new and appetising ways. Star-chef level! Live music Wed and Sat. *Tue–Sat 12pm–3pm, 7pm–10pm | Au Cap | tel. 252 2112 | lgmsey@gmail.com | Expensive*

KAZ KREOL ⛱ (131 E2) *(⌖ H15)*

The small (but excellent) menu offers Creole and international cuisine, their speciality is their famed squid curry. The restaurant is run by an expat couple who are full of helpful hints for your

Seychelles stay. You should reserve well in advance for dinner, as the few places are quickly filled. *Daily | Anse Royale | tel. 437 16 80 | Budget–Moderate*

MAIA LUXURY RESORT & SPA
(128 C6) (*ᗜ F14*)

If you place a lot of value on a couple of thousand square feet of living space, want a butler around the clock and can afford to spare the necessary cash – then this exclusive resort is for you. The 30 private villas offer every comfort imaginable, each with private pool and view of the sea, all set in a unique landscape designed by American architect Bill Bensley. Guests are served meals by a Michelin-starred chef from Taiwan while the young generation enjoy the Jacuzzi or are pampered with chocolate massages. It goes without saying that there is also a magnificent private beach, which is open to the public and an extensive selection of water sports and activities – including ● yoga. *Anse Louis | tel. 439 00 00 | www.maia.com.sc | Expensive*

LE RELAX HOTEL & RESTAURANT ⚜
(131 E2) (*ᗜ H15*)

Small hotel on a hillside with nine lavishly decorated rooms (air-conditioning, TV, mini bar, room service). Great views over the bay, highly recommended restaurant, and a swimming pool. The beach is just a short walk away and offers some excellent snorkelling. *Anse Royale | tel. 438 29 00 | www.lerelaxhotel.com | Budget*

INSIDER TIP VILLA BAMBOU
(130 C1) (*ᗜ F15*)

This small guesthouse is only a few steps away from Anse à la Mouche, one of the most beautiful beaches on Mahé. The three comfortable rooms are beautifully decorated and instead of energy-sapping air-conditioners, fans cool the air.

The rustic guesthouse was built in an environmentally-friendly manner. Breakfast is served in the rooms on request and there are two restaurants in the vicinity. *Anse à la Mouche | Moderate*

VILLAS CHEZ BATISTA
(130 C4) (*ᗜ G17*)

Relaxed hotel with ten tastefully decorated rooms in four bungalows, their position on the stunning beachfront at Anse Takamaka is captivating. The restaurant offers Creole cuisine, especially fresh seafood. *Anse Takamaka | tel. 436 63 00 | www.chezbatista.com | Budget*

LEISURE & SPORTS

In contrast to Beau Vallon Beach, the sports facilities in the southern part of Mahé are mostly limited to those at the hotels. However, most water sports are still possible. Some hotel owners also organise fishing trips; the catch then lands up – deliciously prepared – on the guests' dinner plates.

ENTERTAINMENT

The entertainment in the evenings is usually provided by the larger hotels: folklore shows, Sega music and sometimes a barbecue under the stars.

VICTORIA

▨▨ MAP INSIDE BACK COVER
▨▨ (124 B–C 5–6) (*ᗜ D–E10*) **According to reliable sources, Victoria is the smallest capital in the world, what is certain is that it is the only city in the Seychelles. Its layout makes it hard to distinguish its boundaries, as there is a smooth transition from the centre to the surrounding suburbs.**

VICTORIA

CITY **WHERE TO START?**

Clock Tower: the landmark on the intersection of Independence Avenue, Albert Street and Francis Rachel Street is the meeting point for the capital Victoria. There are shops, banks, agencies, the main post office and the National Museum in the area. Independence Ave leads via Freedom Square, and the Bicentennial Monument, to the harbour.

Victoria is divided into six districts: Bel Air, a part of English River, Mont Fleuri, Mount Buxton, Plaisance and St Louis. About 30,000 people live here – that is slightly more than a third of the total population of the Seychelles. Victoria is of course the seat of the government, houses all the authorities and is thus placed in the centre of public life. The latter takes place mostly on weekdays – on Sundays the little city is usually very quiet and deserted.

The chic suburb of Victoria is ★ ☀ *Bel Air* where there are some magnificent views of Victoria, the harbour area and the outlying islands. From here it is only a few miles on the Sans Souci road to reach *Sans Souci,* where the houses become fewer and the forest denser. The Cypriot Archbishop Makarios took a villa here, a short distance away from the road, as his home in 1956, after he was forced to leave the Mediterranean island for political reasons.

SIGHTSEEING

BOTANICAL GARDENS ★
Founded in 1771, the Botanical Gardens have at least one specimen of all the botanical rarities that grow on the Seychelles. Right at the entrance you can see to the left and right of the path the only impressive coco de mer trees whose female flowers are among the most well-known flowers of palm species. The upper part of the park has largely been left in its natural state. The Botanical Gardens are not only there for leisure activities, there are also various research facilities where scientific experiments with plants are carried out. *Above Mont Fleuri Road | daily 8am–5pm | admission 75 rupees*

CATHEDRAL OF THE IMMACULATE CONCEPTION
If you continue from the market on Church Street in a northerly direction, you will come to the Cathedral of the Immaculate Conception, consecrated in 1874, the largest church in the Seychelles. On Sundays the children born in wedlock are baptised here – on Fridays, those out of wedlock. Since about three quarters of the babies in the Seychelles are born out of wedlock, the priests have their hands full on Fridays. The bells of the corresponding towers reached a certain literary fame. In his novel 'Where the Clock Chimes Twice', the English writer Alec Waugh mentions the whimsical peculiarity of chiming twice on the hour: once at the right time and the second time for the daydreamers and slowcoaches two minutes later *(mass: Mon–Fri 6am, Sat 5pm, Sun 7am and 9am).* Also noteworthy is the imposing two-storey building next to the cathedral, called *La Domus.* It was built out of granite rock in 1934 by Swiss missionaries and today still serves as a residence for Roman Catholic clerics and monks.

MONUMENTS
On the roundabout where Independence and 5th June Avenues meet, is a mod-

ern sculpture, the *Bicentennial Monument*. It is a symbol of the African, Asian and European continents – where most of the Seychellois come from. Also noteworthy is the *Zonm Lib*, the stylized statue of a man who holds the broken chains of slavery in his hands *(on 5th June Ave-*

quite hard to decipher. It is said there are some pirates' graves here. Perhaps you will find Louis Poiret's grave, he claimed to be the legitimate son of the deposed Louis XVI and therefore the lost King of France, a claim since refuted by scientists through genetic tests.

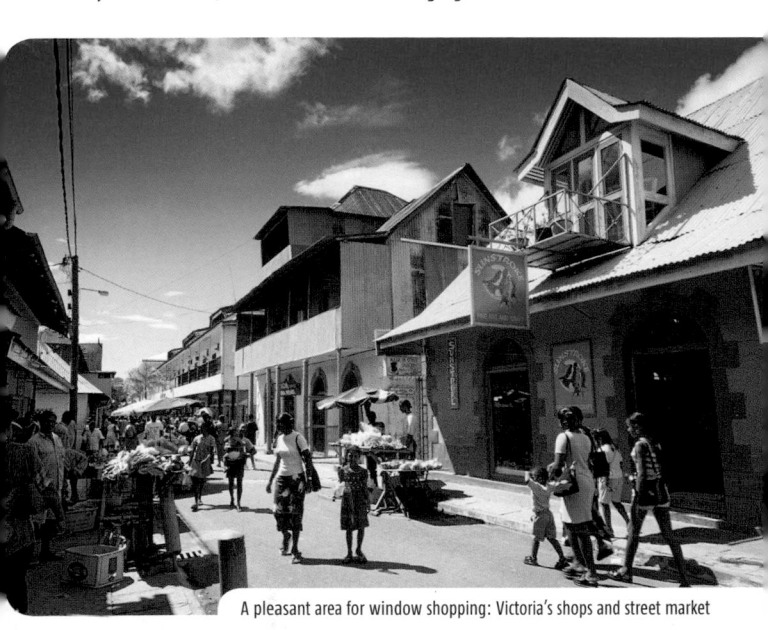

A pleasant area for window shopping: Victoria's shops and street market

nue). The statue was created by a local artist on the occasion of the Seychelles' Declaration of Independence; it was inaugurated in 1978 and dedicated to the martyrs who rebelled against colonisation and oppression on 5 June 1977.

BEL AIR CEMETERY ★
From Revolution Avenue head south and then turn into Bel Air Road and after a short walk you reach the suburb of Bel Air. On the left hand side lies the Bel Air Cemetery which was restored a few years ago. Unfortunately the inscriptions on the weathered tombstones are

GRAND TRIANON
This colonial style house on Revolution Avenue once housed a famous guest: in his search for his colleague David Livingstone, the British explorer of Africa, Henry Morton Stanley, made this a stopover (1841–1904). Today the building houses the highly recommended *Marie Antoinette* restaurant *(see 'Food & Drink')*.

ARUL MIHU NAVASAKTHI VINAYAGAR HINDU TEMPLE ●
The only Hindu temple in the Seychelles is not far from the centre of Victoria. The ornate and colourful temple was

built in 1992 and named after Vinaya-gar, the god of safety and prosperity. It is worth paying attention to the gate tower that is richly decorated with Hindu deities, called Gopuram. *Quincy Street | daily 6am–midday and 5pm–9pm | admission free*

INSIDER TIP **KENWYN HOUSE** ●

If you are interested in Seychelles art, you will find something here. Kenwyn House, a historic wooden building, offers a gallery, where works by artists living in the Seychelles are exhibited. The building itself is an exceptional exam-

and vibrant. One floor is reserved for a South African jewellery retailer and the valuable items (pearls, diamonds) are exempt from VAT. *Francis Rachel Street | Mon–Fri 9am–5pm, Sat 9am–1pm | admission free | www.kenwynhouse.com*

NATIONAL LIBRARY BUILDING/ NATIONAL ARCHIVES ●

Those interested in the history, geography and literature of the Seychelles, will find lots of interesting information here. Since 1995 the surprisingly rich national archive has been located in this modern glass and steel building not far from the

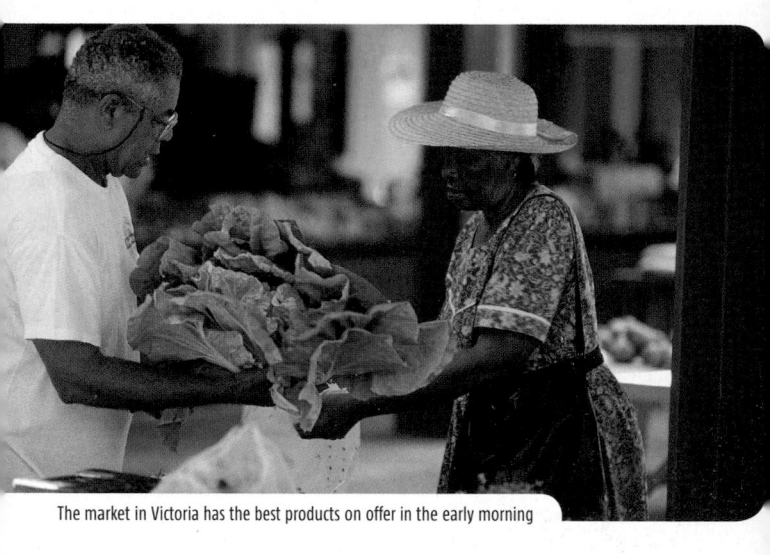

The market in Victoria has the best products on offer in the early morning

ple of 19th century colonial architecture and served as the seat for the telephone company Cable & Wireless for a long time, before it was converted into an exclusive souvenir shop. There is also an art exhibition of paintings and needless to say the works of Sir Michael Adams are also on display. The works by other artists such as George Camille and Barbara Jenson are just as colourful

centre of Victoria. The reading room is pleasantly air-conditioned and the staff are happy to inform visitors on specific topics. *Francis Rachel Street | Mon–Fri 8.30am–3.30pm, Sat 8.30am–midday | admission free*

NATIONAL MUSEUM ★ ●

Just behind the Clock Tower on Francis Rachel Street lies the National Museum of the Seychelles. It provides a good insight into the history of the archipelago. On display are documents and historical nautical charts, weapons and cannons, model boats and traditional musical instruments. You can also find the *Possession Stone* here that was laid by Captain Nicolas Morphey in 1756. Regular temporary art exhibitions take place in the National Museum. *State House Avenue | Mon/Tue, Thu/Fri 8.30am–4.30pm, Wed 8.30am–midday, Sat 9am–1pm | admission 15 rupees*

SIR SELWYN SELWYN CLARKE MARKET ★ ●

If you visit Victoria on a Saturday morning, it is worth your while to take a stroll through the *Sir Selwyn Selwyn Clarke Market*. It is slightly set back on Albert Street, only a short walk from the Clock Tower. In order to experience it in all its diversity, you should get up as early as the Seychellois. They start arriving there at 7am to do their weekend shopping because that is when the best variety is on offer; it is also fun to browse in the shops around the market. Perhaps you will find a pretty gift for those back home in the motley mix of goods on offer. It is best to have plenty of coins on hand as most of the traders don't have change for larger denominations. *Albert Street | Mon–Fri 7am–5.30pm, Sat 6am–2pm*

CITY CENTRE

To dispel a common misconception: the *Clock Tower*, a prominent orientation point near the end of Independence Avenue, is not a miniature version of Big Ben, but of the clock tower at Vauxhall Bridge in London. It was a gift from the British government, erected in 1903, when the Seychelles took the first step towards independence. There is a lot of activity on weekdays around the

clock tower. Not far from there are several wooden houses with souvenir vendors selling arts and crafts made in the Seychelles, as well as a large number of other shops, boutiques, banks and travel agencies. The main post office is also found here. If you turn left into Francis Rachel Street, you will see the pretty, INSIDERTIP colourful colonial style wooden houses.

ST PAUL'S CATHEDRAL

On 14 May 1859 the first Anglican Bishop of Mauritius, Vincent William Ryan, consecrated the cathedral on Revolution Avenue, which is the Anglican parish church of Victoria. In 1920, when the British abolished the entire government of Mauritius and the Seychelles, it became the Bishop's official secondary residence. Its modern appearance today is a result of alterations and extensions done between 2001 and 2004. Today it can accommodate about 800 worshippers. *Mass: Mon midday, Tue 6.30am, Wed 9am, Thu 5.30am, Fri 6.30am and midday, Sat 5pm and Sun 6.30am and 8.30am*

FOOD & DRINK

BEL AIR

You need to make a timely reservation because this restaurant only has a few tables. It belongs to the Hotel Bel Air hotel and was completely renovated in 2012. There is no menu as the service is a buffet. The flavours are all uniquely Creole, the ingredients very fresh as the chef shops daily at the market. *Only for lunch, closed Sun | Bel Air Road | tel. 422 44 16 | Budget*

INSIDERTIP MARIE ANTOINETTE ●

What's special about this restaurant is the fact that there is only one (changes daily) Creole lunch and evening menu. Menus are therefore unnecessary, but you can still select individual items from the menu. Reservations essential! *Closed Sun | Grand Trianon | Revolution Avenue | tel. 426 62 22 | Moderate*

PIRATES ARMS ●
See and be seen: relax on the terrace – which faces the road – and indulge in some people watching as you observe the hustle and bustle around the Clock Tower in Victoria's centre. Culinary it is nothing special but there are reasonably priced snacks and refreshing drinks. Next door is a shopping arcade with a few small shops selling attractive souvenirs and there is also antique dealer. *Daily | Independence Avenue | tel. 422 50 01 | Budget*

SAM'S PIZZERIA
If you are longing for some Italian cuisine, this is your best bet. Even Italian guests consider these pizzas, which are baked in a stone oven, the best pizzas south of Sicily. But since there are also those who want to try something different, they also serve home cooked Creole dishes. *Daily | Francis Rachel Street | tel. 432 24 99 | Budget*

SPORTS & ACTIVITIES

The wide bay of Victoria lends itself to sailing and you can hire a boat from the *Marine Charter Association*. It is also possible to charter yachts without a crew. The only golf course on Mahé the *Reef Golf Club* in Anse aux Pins *(south*

FOR BOOKWORMS AND FILM BUFFS

Seychelles – The Best of: a beautiful coffee table book by international photographer Gregor Kervina that is a photographic journey of the pristine Inner Islands and their exquisite and unique nature. The book is available online from www.seychellesbest.com

Seychelles – Encyclopaedia of the Underwater World – This book by Vincenzo Paolillo may be a little dated but there is no better compendium about the impressive underwater world of the islands.

Wildlife of Seychelles – A book by John Bowler that is an excellent photographic guide to all the fauna and flora of the Seychelles, lots of colourful wildlife pictures.

The Seychelles Affair – This non-fiction book by mercenary Mike Hoare is an account of his abortive coup attempt (funded by the South African intelligence service) and his prosecution and subsequent imprisonment in a South African jail.

TV/Cinema – the Seychelles is repeatedly used as a scenic backdrop for glamorous TV series, commercials and stills shoots: commercial directors swear by the picturesque boulders of La Digue and the secluded coves of Praslin.

For Your Eyes Only – A collection of short stories by Ian Fleming featuring British Secret Service spy James Bond. One of the stories is set in the Seychelles.

Colonial architecture in Victoria: Marie Antoinette restaurant

of the airport, 9 holes), is open to non-members and visitors need only pay the green fee. In Mont Fleuri there is a squash court at the Polytechnic as well as one in North East Point.

HIKING ON MAHÉ ★

On Mahé there are a number of hiking trails with varying degrees of difficulty. The nature walks and trails are generally well maintained and are usually signposted so well that you cannot get lost. This is why you should follow the signs and not deviate from the path if you are not sure of the way. Be careful: in wet weather you should avoid longer hikes when the trails tend to get slippery! It is also advisable to let your hotel reception know the hike that you intend to take.

Some of the recommended trails on Mahé include the following: hike in the *Morne Seychellois National Park* along the rocky north-west coast of Mahé up to the small bay of Anse Major *(duration: there and back approx. 3 hrs / degree of difficulty: easy)*. The *Vacoa Nature Trail* starts at the end of La Misère

Road, leads up and around the Dauban River, where you will have to cross several bridges, you'll also see the tall Seychelles screw pine trees *(duration: there and back approx. 1 hr / degree of difficulty: easy)*. A demanding hike, which should only be undertaken if you are relatively fit, is the five hour hike up ⋙ *Morne Blanc;* you will also need proper hiking shoes and weatherproof clothing. It is mostly a steep uphill climb but the rewards are worth it: magnificent views over the west coast of Mahé. On the way you can make a stopover at the **INSIDER TIP** *Tea Factory (Mon–Fri 7am–4pm / tel. 437 82 21),* the only tea factory in the Seychelles (established in 1962), where you can take a guided tour (tickets 23 rupees) for information about the tea production, and then have a cup of tea afterwards. You can also buy the tea, of course...

At the *National Parks & Forestry Section* in Victoria's Botanical Gardens, you can get brochures detailing a total of 13 different hikes. The booklets don't cost much, but are sometimes out of stock.

ENTERTAINMENT

The Seychellois use to go to bed early and it was only with the increase in tourism that the nightlife slowly developed, and the local youth are now also joining in. The popular discos are *Tequila Boom (Beau Belle | Victo-*

WHERE TO STAY

There are no large hotels in Victoria, but instead there are charming guesthouses, often family run and with good local cuisine. Large hotels and resorts can be found under 'North Point/Beau Vallon' and 'Southern Mahé'.

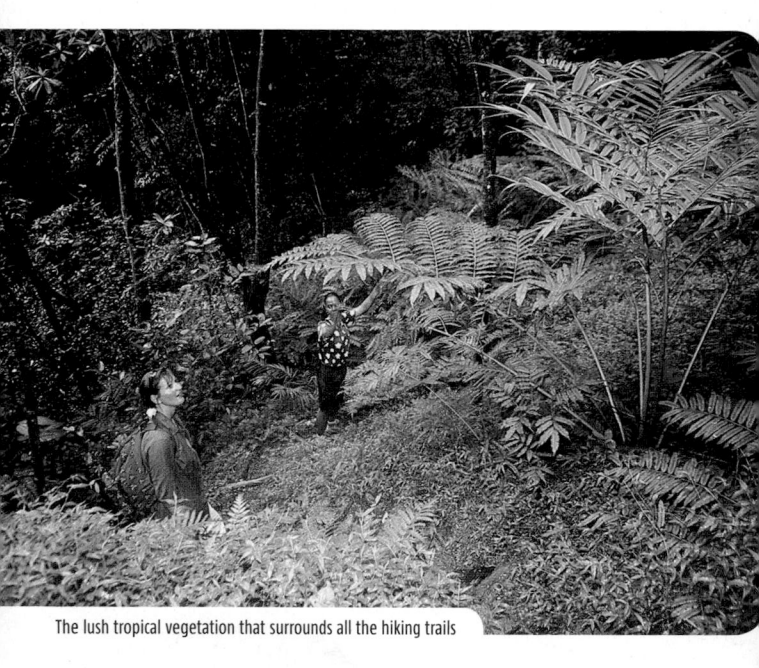

The lush tropical vegetation that surrounds all the hiking trails

ria | Wed, Fri, Sat 10pm–6am) and the open air disco, *Katiolo,* at Anse Faure *(Wed, Fri, Sat from 9pm)*. In the larger hotels on the island there is usually an organised entertainment programme. A popular meeting place especially for younger Seychellois is the bar INSIDER TIP ▶ *Board Walk* in the harbour on Eden Island, on Friday evenings the party is on. Mahé also has casinos – the most popular are in the Hotel Kempinski and at the Berjaya Beau Vallon Bay Beach Resort.

BEAU SÉJOUR �△

This small colonial style guesthouse is set in a gorgeous tropical garden. Nestled at the foot of a mountain, is has great views of Victoria harbour and the islands of the marine parks. Its 9 rooms are tastefully decorated yet still quite reasonably priced. On request the owners organise excursions to Mahé and the neighbouring islands. Only bed and breakfast, no restaurant. *Curio Road Bel Air | tel. 422 61 44 | beausejour_sey@ yahoo.com | Budget*

HOTEL BEL AIR ⚬

A simple but comfortable guesthouse, in an old colonial mansion, with just seven air-conditioned rooms. Beautiful views over Victoria. *Bel Air | tel. 422 44 16 | www.seychelles.net/belair | Budget*

INFORMATION

There is a Seychelles Tourism Board office on Mahé:

SEYCHELLES TOURIST OFFICE

Bel Ombre | P.O. Box 1262 | Victoria | Mahé | tel. 4671300 | www.seychelles. travel

TOURIST INFORMATION OFFICE CITY CENTRE

Independence House | Independence Avenue | Victoria | Mon–Fri 8am–4.30pm, Sat 9am–midday | tel. 4 610800

ISLANDS IN THE VICINITY

Seven islands lie off the coast of Victoria Bay; together they form the *Ste Anne Marine National Park.* The designation of the islands as a nature reserve and the concomitant regulations of the maritime traffic were a matter of real urgency because the propellers of the ships entering and leaving Victoria unfortunately caused damage to the once magnificent underwater world. It is now a popular nature destination.

ANONYME

(129 E–F2) (*🗺 H12*)

This private island with and area of nearly 25 acres is located right in front of the airport on Mahé's east coast. Its location sounds worse than it is, because the air traffic is comparatively low. Large passenger planes only take off and land a few times a day. The *Ano-*

nyme Resort changed hands in 2010 and the luxury resort that was previously on the island, as well as the restaurant, have since closed down. You can however, take a boat from Mahé and go to the island at high tide, which is what most of the local families do on weekends so that they can spend the day there swimming. When the tide is low you can wade the short distance to the island. The crystal clear waters off the island are ideal for snorkelling.

CERF ISLAND ★

(117 E–F6) (*🗺 F–G 10–11*)

Only 5 km/3.1 mi from Victoria, the island of Cerf is worth a visit just for its gorgeous beaches but it is also home to ● Caspar and Caroline, two old giant tortoises, who will patiently allow you to pet them. With its approximately 300 acres the island is about the same size as Bird and Denis and it was named after the French expedition ship 'Le Cerf', which had the famous Possession Stone on board.

The local tour operators offer excursion programmes which include barbecues on the beach, a meal at a restaurant or the opportunity to snorkel in the waters of the National Park. If you don't participate in an organised trip, you should reserve a table at *Kapok Tree (tel. 432 29 59 | Moderate)* or at *Restaurant aux Frères de la Côté (tel. 432 47 49 | Moderate)* and inquire about the ferries that pick up guests to and from the harbour in Mahé. You can stay overnight at *L'Habitation des Cerfs (14 rooms | tel. 432 3111 | www.seyvillas.com/hotel-habitation | Budget)* on the north coast or in the more exclusive, but also more expensive *Cerf Island Resort (12 rooms | tel. 429 45 00 | www.cerf-resort.com | Moderate)* on the south coast.

LONG ISLAND (125 F5–6) *(🗺 G10)*

Long Island was once used as a quarantine station for female leprosy patients. The island has been unpopulated since the closure of the station. Now, a luxury retreat is planned for spa guests that should be under management of the international Shangri-La hotel chain. Strict environmental rulings must be complied with here, so far this has prevented more building. No final completion date was available at the time of going to press.

MOYENNE ISLAND (125 F5) *(🗺 G10)*

The granite island of Moyenne, which measures less than 250 acres, is Volcanic. Since 1970 it has been part of the protected Ste Anne Marine National Park, and since 2009 an independent park known as Moyenne Island National Park. The island was privately owned by the native Englishman and former Australian newspaper publisher Brendan Grimshaw. He purchased the island in 1962 for about £ 8,000. He also gained the revenue from the small restaurant *Jolly Roger* as a bonus.

Since Grimshaw died in 2012, the island has remained uninhabited and visitors are only permitted as part of organised tours from Mahé. There is no overnight accommodation.

Grimshaw not only looked after the hiking trails around most of the island, but also more than 100 giant tortoises that live here. These are considered to be the world's largest cohesive population of their kind. Many bird species are also found here – the island is considered to be a sanctuary for numerous endemic bird species, while more than 150 fish varieties were counted on the coral reefs. Moyenne's beaches are amongst the most beautiful on the Seychelles; you can also go snorkelling and enjoy amazing glimpses of the island's marine life. Apart from several ruins of old buildings, there are also two graves on the island. These are thought to contain the mortal remains of pirates. Rumour has it that the legendary treasure of the pirate Labuse is hidden here. Also worth seeing is a quaint chapel built of timber.

ROUND ISLAND (125 F5) *(🗺 G10)*

Lazare Picault discovered the island and named it 'round island' as it only measures 200 m/656 ft in diameter. Visitors only used to be "allowed" here, if they had done something wrong – Long Island was the prison island of the Seychelles. Since 2013, Round Island has a luxury hotel – the *Enchanted Island Resort* (tel. 00971 48 14 56 78 | www.

THE GAUGUIN OF THE SEYCHELLES

● Even if you cannot afford an original a visit to Michael Adams – the 'Gauguin of the Seychelles' – is almost obligatory. If the expat Englishman is not busy travelling the world opening one of his many exhibitions, you may get to meet the down to earth artist himself.

His house on Mahé – with a small exhibition room where you can buy inexpensive prints – is just before Anse à la Mouche at Anse aux Poules Bleues *(Mon–Fri 10am–4pm | tel. 436 10 06)*. Works by Michael Adams now hang in many prestigious art galleries around the world.

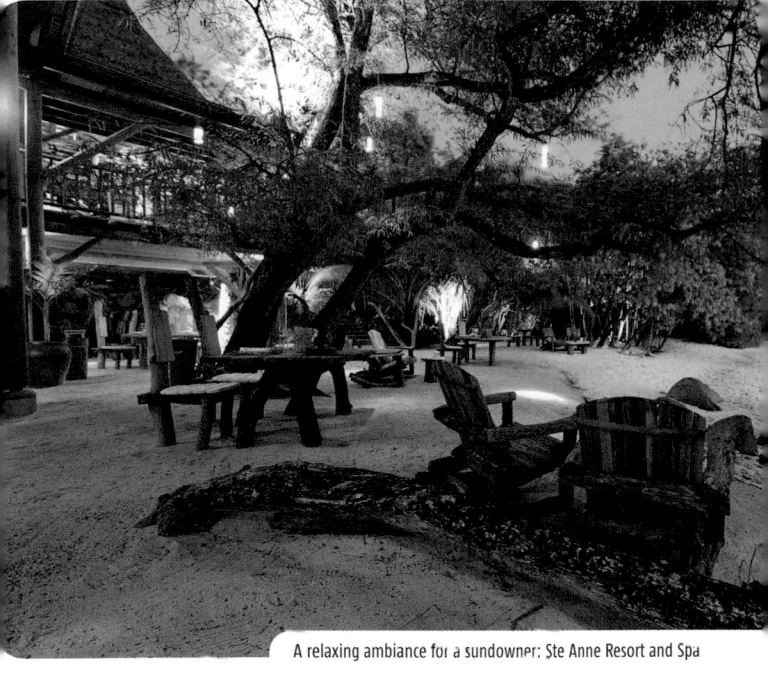

A relaxing ambiance for a sundowner: Ste Anne Resort and Spa

jaresortshotels.com | Expensive) with ten colonial-style villas where every comfort is provided for. All villas have private pools and direct beach access. There is a pool-side restaurant Bounty. If you prefer more privacy, you can enjoy the butler service in your villa. Prices for overnight stays are from 13,800 rupees per villa, per day.

STE ANNE ISLAND
(125 E–F4) *(ɷ G9)*
Ste Anne has a surface area of about 500 acres and is the namesake island of the Ste Anne Marine National Park. It has some historical interest because it was the first island in the archipelago that was settled by people. However, it is its other inhabitants that have aroused the interest of biologists: Ste Anne is a favourite nesting site for hawksbill turtles. From 1983 to 2001 the island was off limits but at the end of 2002 a five star hotel was opened by the Mauritian Beachcomber Group. The luxury *Sainte Anne Resort and Spa (tel. 429 20 00 | www.beachcomber-ho tels.com/sainte-anne-resort.php | Expensive)* has 87 private villas, some with private swimming pools. Facilities include a wellness centre with spa, sauna and massages as well as two tennis courts with floodlights, all befitting a hotel of this standard. As the island is in a nature reserve, water sports are limited to non-motorised activities. The resort includes a bar and five restaurants, such as the *Le Mont Fleuri* with Italian cuisine or the *L'Abondance*. Packages are all-inclusive.

PRASLIN AND NEIGH-BOURING ISLANDS

According to travel connoisseurs, the true Seychelles are to be found when you leave the main island of Mahé, and travel to the other beautiful islands.

This is true in one sense but also not entirely true in another: while Mahé does have a well developed tourist infrastructure is still has some of what the other islands have to offer and if you choose Mahé as a holiday destination, you can always make INSIDER TIP ▶ day trips to the neighbouring islands.

ARIDE

(0) (ΩΩ K–L1) All the things that money can buy: in 1973 the Scottish aristocrat and chocolate manufacturer Christopher Cadbury (1909–86) acquired the small (170 acre) granitic island of Aride, home to one million endemic sea birds.

He bought the island as a reserve for the *Royal Society for the Promotion of Nature Conservation* and served as the society's president until his death. In 2004 the *Island Conservation Society* took over the island's management and opened a nature conservation centre on Aride, where ornithologists research the world of birds. With conservation the island now has the ideal conditions for breeding and five bird species – once considered extinct – have returned *(www.aride island.com)*. Now the birds can breed, lay their eggs and raise their young undisturbed. There are over a million sea birds (including the rare Noddy and

Millions of birds can't be wrong: travel beyond Mahé and discover the pristine natural beauty of the Seychelles

Roseate Terns, Great Frigatebird and the White-tailed Tropicbird) that return here every year. Ten different bird species were counted by an ornithologist commissioned by the Seychelles government. ● Whilst he had access to the island at any time, tourists are only able to access Aride from Mondays to Fridays and only with an organised excursion, the weather must also be fair enough to make the landing in the small boats. The journey takes about two hours from Mahé (50 km/31.1 mi) and about 40 minutes from Praslin (10 km/6.2 mi). There is no regular boat traffic.

Aride is the northernmost of the granite islands on the Seychelles Plateau and was discovered by Captain Nicolas Morphey in 1756. The name it carries today alludes to its climate: hot and dry. About a dozen inhabitants live in a small settlement on the island; they earn a living from the sale of guano.

Aride has a lush, tropical landscape with a great variety of plants. The guano enriched soil of the island is extremely fertile, evidenced by the fruits that grow here, such as lemons, oranges, bananas, and spices such as cinnamon, ginger and vanilla. There is a pathway for visitors (do not leave the designated route) that was

The skink, a glimmering resident of Cousin Island

designed to lead past all the interesting places with good viewpoints. Areas that are off limits (e.g. turtle nesting sites on the beach) are signposted. A nice nature

trail also takes you up to the top ⚘ of the 135 m/443 ft high hill where you will emerge from the woodland to have a magnificent panoramic view.

Another attraction (despite the coral bleaching events of 1998) is the ★ *underwater world off Aride.* A short time ago divers counted no fewer than 88 different species of fish during a single 90 minute dive. But even while just snorkelling you will get an excellent impression of the colourful underwater landscape.

There is no hotel or restaurant on Aride. Visitors bring a packed lunch along and enjoy a picnic instead. The picnic hut is also the only place where smoking is allowed on the island! You can only visit Aride with an organised tour group *(Mon–Fri | bookings via hotels or travel operators in Victoria)*. The fee including guided tour is about 770 rupees per person.

COUSIN

(0) *(⌖ K6)* **The tiny (only 70 acres) granite island of Cousin – not to be confused with the island of Cousine – is one of the last sanctuaries for bird species threatened with extinction.**

In 1968 the International Council for Bird Preservation bought the island and with the aid of World Wild Life Fund for Nature (WWF) made it into a nature reserve, one that is unique even for the Seychelles. The first goal was relatively easy to attain: to protect the few remaining specimens of the decimated Seychelles Warbler and Seychelles Weaver from extinction. This was a conservation success and populations of both birds can now be found on several of the nearby islands.

Today a lot is being done to return this almost circular island, that was once a dense deciduous forest, back to its original state. Man's sensitive intervention can be seen in the results yielded by nature: several dozen bird species now breed here. Cousin is also one of the best protected breeding grounds for hawksbill turtles in the world, has the highest density of lizards and even has a few giant tortoises. The best time for a trip to Cousin is during April or May, when hundreds of thousands of seabirds come here to breed. There are a number of rules to be aware of on your visit to Cousin: do not stray from the designated pathways or remove anything from the island, all waste must be taken back with you, smoking is not permitted and it goes without saying that the birds and other wildlife should not be disturbed. Staying over on the island is also off limits!

The distance from Mahé is 44 km/27.3 mi so it is better to visit Cousin from Praslin or La Digue, where travel agencies and hotels organise the trips. Visitors are only allowed on the island from Mon–Fri between 9.30am–midday (closed weekends and public holidays), the boats go as close as they can to the island and then you have to transfer to a private island boat. The landing fee is about 385 rupees per person.

COUSINE

(0) (*J–K7*) **This is another island that attaches great importance to nature conservation. This small (60 acre) private island is one of the smallest granite islands and is home to a dozen specimens of the Seychelles White-rumped Shama and other very rare endemic birds.**

Hawksbill turtles also lay their eggs on Cousine, on the east coast the island has a very long sandy beach and from September to January the waters around the island have some excellent snorkelling.

You can stay overnight at the ⚲ *Cousine Island Resort* (about 23,000 rupees per night, helicopter transfer from Mahé approx. 15 min | www.cousineisland.com | *Expensive*). This complex that consists of only four French colonial villas can accommodate a maximum ten guests. The minimum stay is three nights and included in the room rate is a sapling which you can plant in a selected spot. On request the local conservation officer will take guests around the island and

---

explain the nature conservation initiatives. The resort has a swimming pool and a library and this is the ideal place for those looking for peace and pure relaxation.

LA DIGUE

(135 D–F 1–3) (📖 S–T 6–8) When you first leave the small harbour of Praslin, the powerful diesel engine drives the boat on but then the wind fills up the white sails. The crossing is a small taste of what awaits the visitor on La Digue – peace and calm.

its visitors. On La Digue there is no hustle and bustle – everything has its own very leisurely pace. Ox wagons used to be the mode of transportation for people and goods on La Digue. Nowadays, they are not seen so often, although sometimes they are still used for short island tours and are available for hire. Today there are also – perhaps regrettably – a greater number of taxis, which race through the narrow island streets.

Lazare Picault discovered La Digue in 1744 and named the island *Île Rouge* (red island) because of its reddish granite rocks. In 1768 the French captain and explorer, Marion Dufresne, gave the fourth largest

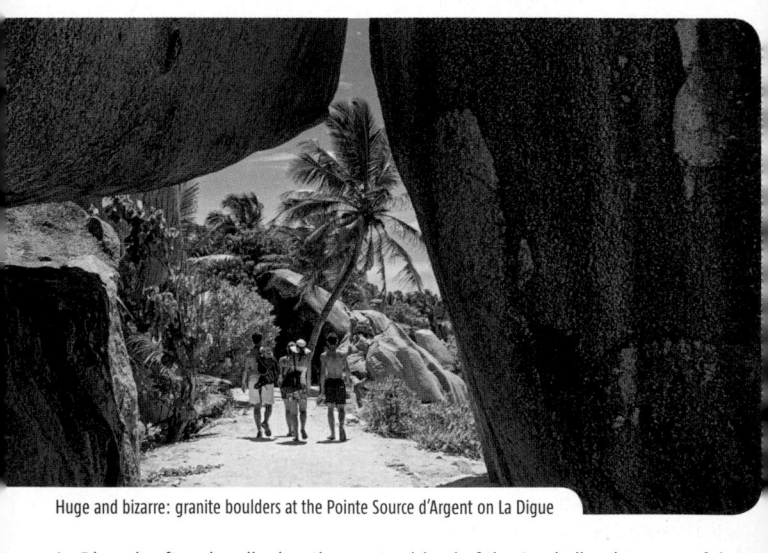

Huge and bizarre: granite boulders at the Pointe Source d'Argent on La Digue

La Digue is often described as the most beautiful island in the Seychelles, and its many small, hidden coves and fine sandy beaches are well known around the world as the backdrop to countless advertisements. On the coast there are pristine beaches fringed by gigantic rock boulders, in the interior there are lush tropical plants – a package that captivates all

island of the Seychelles the name of the command ship in his expedition armada. About 2,200 people live on La Digue – and not only from tourism. The island has fertile soil, where coconut trees and aromatic plants (such as vanilla) thrive. There is no flight connection between Mahe and La Digue the closest airport is located on Praslin. Flights take place several times a day. From Praslin there are two high-speed catamarans that run daily trips to La Digue and they only take about 30 minutes to cover the short distance.

SIGHTSEEING

ISLAND ROUND TRIP ★

La Digue is only about 4 mi² so it is best to explore the island by bicycle. A complete island circumnavigation is not possible, however, as there is vegetation and some steep cliffs. In some places you may need to get off and push the bike. If it gets too hard you can always turn around. However, once you do get through the dense vegetation it opens up to the sea and you'll be rewarded with views over the 🌊 magnificent landscape with smooth granite boulders. The rocks tower up to 330 m/1,083 ft *(access via the L'Union Estate coconut farm).* You can also find small, magical bays with white coral sand when you head south-east on the road from La Passe. At this end you will find the beaches *Grand' Anse, Petite Anse, Anse Songe* and INSIDERTIP *Grand l'Anse.*

POINTE SOURCE D'ARGENT/ ANSE LA SOURCE À JEAN
(135 E3) *(𝄢 S8)*

The mighty ★ *granite rocks* at the Pointe Source d'Argent could quite possibly be the most photographed boulders on earth and they feature in just about all of the advertisements for the Seychelles. Right behind them is *La Source à Jean,* a beach with pristine sand and crystal clear water. *Daily 7am–5pm | admission about 150 rupees*

L'UNION ESTATE
(135 E2) *(𝄢 S8)*

From the ferry pier it is only a short walk south to the farm estate. It was bought in the 1970s by a German, Herbert Mittermayer. For many years he was considered a benefactor by the inhabitants of La Digue. He built a harbour jetty and an island hospital and had an irrigation system installed but in 1980 the estate was expropriated by President France Albert René. Today the farm currently provides jobs for 350 workers and during the week *(9am–4pm | 150 rupees)* there are demonstrations about the commercial use of coconuts such as the extraction of oil from coconut flesh. The farm also has air-conditioned chalets (with half board) that are located right on a beautiful beach *(info/bookings: www. ladigue.sc | Moderate).*

On the property there is also the recently renovated *Plantation House*, a fine example of French colonial architecture. It was built by a family, who came from Mauritius to the Seychelles and made their fortune by cultivating coconuts and spices. The house is open to the public *(Mon–Fri | around 75 rupees),* it is built with rare wood and has a roof traditionally thatched with palm leaves.

FOOD & DRINK

BERNIQUE (135 E2) *(𝄢 S7)*

The restaurant belongs to the Bernique guesthouse. It is an attractive establishment serving local cuisine; on occasion they also have a Creole buffet. *Daily lunch and dinner | La Passe | tel. 423 42 29 | Budget*

THE VEUVE (135 E2) *(𝄢 S7)*

The hotel restaurant, which belongs to the La Digue Island Lodge serves (expensive) local and international cuisine. Occasionally a buffet is set up or a barbecue is organised. Nice bar with a great atmosphere. *Anse de la Réunion | tel. 423 42 32 | Expensive*

ZEROF
(135 E2) *(⟨ S7)*

Thanks to the delicious Creole cuisine it is also a favourite meeting place amongst the locals. *Daily 8am–10pm | Anse de la Réunion | tel. 423 44 39 | Budget*

ENTERTAINMENT

There is none of the usual organised evening entertainment on La Digue. After the sun sets (Anse de la Réunion is the ideal spot) you simply sit at the bar and sip an obligatory sundowner. As only a few streets are lit, you should remember to take your torch.

WHERE TO STAY

BERNIQUE GUESTHOUSE
(135 E2) *(⟨ S7)*

Well maintained guesthouse set in the midst of a coconut grove, with six pretty rooms. Anse la Passe beach is about a 15 minute walk away. The owner orga-nises INSIDER TIP excursions for sea angling. *La Passe | tel. 423 45 18 | www.berniqueguesthouse.com | Budget*

CALOU GUESTHOUSE
(135 E2) *(⟨ S7)*

This is a relaxed guesthouse. The restaurant serves Creole cuisine, there is also a bar, bicycle rental and boat trips. *5 rooms | La Passe | tel. 423 40 83 | www.calouguesthouse.com | Budget*

CHÂTEAU ST CLOUD **(135 E2)** *(⟨ S7)*

A small, elegant hotel dating back 100 years, the sixth generation of the family now run the hotel. It has 3 categories of spacious rooms in a beautiful tropical garden with tortoises. A small pool with a waterwall shower. *La Réunion | tel. 423 43 46 | www.chateaustcloud.sc | Moderate*

LA DIGUE ISLAND LODGE
(135/E2) *(⟨ S7)*

For years this was the first hotel on the square with all the usual facilities like a

Overnight stays in the resort on Frégate are pricey, but it's an exclusive pleasure

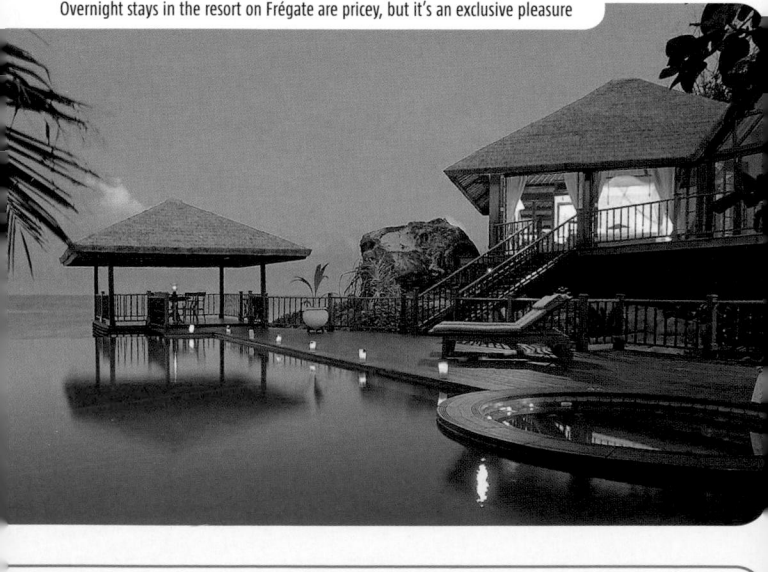

pool, bar, restaurant, diving area, ● bicycle rental. While its slightly old-fashioned, its unique location by the beach is outstanding and its just a stones throw from the *Union Estate* with access to Anse Source d'Argent. There are 60 palm thatched chalets that are pleasant and comfortable as well as nine more rooms in *La Maison Jaune,* a colonial building built around the 1900s. The in-house restaurant, *The Veuve,* offers excellent cuisine. *Anse de la Réunion | tel. 423 42 32 | www.ladigue.sc | Expensive*

DOMAINE DE L'ORANGERAIE
(135 E1) (*M S6*)
A paradise hotel complex: small tropical villas at the heart of an exotic garden; friendly and professional service, a fine spa area, pool bar and luxury restaurant, delicious food and a menu with several courses, although rather pricey. *63 bungalows| La Passe | Anse Sévère | tel. 429 99 99 | www.orangeraie.sc | Expensive*

PATATRAN VILLAGE
(135 E1) (*M S6*)
Attractive hotel with 18 comfortable bungalows idyllically located on a slope overlooking a small, picturesque bay. Traditional Diguois island dishes are served in the restaurant, once a week there is a delicious Creole buffet. *Anse Patates | tel. 429 43 00 | patatran@seychelles.net | Budget–Moderate*

ISLANDS IN THE VICINITY

North-east of La Digue are four small islands, one of them, *Félicité* (O) (*M U6*), was home to the Malayan Sultan of Perak who was exiled there in the 19th century for five years. Since 2016 this private island, which is only 3 km/1.9 mi from La Digue, has an exclusive hotel complex

(Zil Pasyon | www.sixsenses.com | Moderate–Expensive) with six luxury mansions. Tennis, scuba diving, snorkelling and swimming are on offer, the restaurant serves exceptional Creole and international cuisine. The other islands surrounding La Digue include *Grande Sœur* (O) (*M U4*), *Petite Sœur* (O) (*M T4*) and *Marianne* (O) (*M W6–7*). You can reach Félicité and Marianne by boat from La Digue, the other islands from Praslin. Between Félicité and Grande Sœur lie three uninhabited islets: *Île Cocos, Île Platte* and *Île La Fouche.*

FRÉGATE

(135 E–F 4–5) (*M G–H 4–5*) This charming little granite island was once the preferred hideout of pirates but today the exclusive Hotel Frégate Island Private with 16 villas (opened in 1998) is one of the most expensive hotels in the Seychelles.

The island belongs to a wealthy German industrialist who not only values exclusivity but also protects and nurtures the environment, especially the last of the remaining Seychelles White-rumped Shama, making it popular with nature and bird lovers.

The island was named by Lazare Picault after the abundance of Great Frigatebirds (they have a wingspan of up to 2 m/6.6 ft) he found there on his second expedition in 1744. In the dense interior of the island there is an **INSIDER TIP** extraordinary diversity of plants and a large number of rare birds, the reason why Frégate has become a desired destination for ornithologists from all over the world. In 2012 the arrival of the Seychelles Warbler – a small songbird that only exists on four other islands on the Seychelles – marked the 100th bird species to make its home on Frégate. Throughout the year there are about 40 ecologists and ornithologists working with the nature conservation on Frégate. They also offer guided ornithological hikes across the island. After a half hour walk you reach the ⚡ *Mont Signale*, the highest point of the island, with a wonderful view.

And if you are looking for your dream beach, you will find it on Frégate. There are no fewer than seven of them here. South of the *Plantation House* lies *Anse Parc*, which is a wonderful place to snorkel at high tide, and in the opposite direction is ★ *Anse Victorin,* probably the most beautiful beach on Frégate. On the northern end of the airstrip is *Anse Bambou*, a beautiful small bay with white coral sand (warning: sometimes there are dangerous currents!). A nice walk leads to the opposite end of the island and to *Grand' Anse,* also a great snorkelling area at high tide. There is the great likelihood of coming across some of the island's 2,200 giant tortoises on the way.

FOOD & DRINK/ WHERE TO STAY

FRÉGATE ISLAND PRIVATE
With only 16 villas and prices of 67,600 rupees per night the hotel (which opened in 1998) is one of the most exclusive facilities on the Seychelles. Each villa has an area of more than 2,000 ft² and a private swimming pool, and there are two expensive restaurants and a spa. Bookings *www.fregate.com* | *Expensive*

LEISURE & SPORTS

To snorkel you can either stroll to *Grand' Anse* or to *Anse Parc,* where there are still many INSIDER TIP intact coral reefs to explore. There is also a wide variety of water sports on offer.

PRASLIN

(132–133) *(𝄞 L–Q 4–7)* **The Vallée de Mai National Park on Praslin Island is an exceptional natural wonder, even by the rich natural beauty standards of the Seychelles, and if you miss out on a visit you will miss out on one of the greatest attractions of the Indian Ocean archipelago.**

With an area of just 7 mi², it is certainly not a giant amongst the world's national parks, but unlike any other it offers a dense concentration of the different plants typical to the Seychelles. This is what most of the islands of this archipelago must have looked like before the first Europeans settled on the Seychelles and set about intervening in the unspoilt nature that flourished here. No one knows why this valley was spared; it may well be the impenetrable vegetation or its seclusion deep in the island's interior. Whatever the reason – this large expanse of million-year old natural forest has remained almost entirely untouched. And there is hope that this strictly conserved area will preserve its state and appearance in the future. The Vallée de Mai with its unique coco de mer palm forest is one of the smallest areas to be declared a World Heritage Site by Unesco.

Praslin, with a length of 12 km/7.5 mi and a maximum width of 5 km/3.1 mi, is the second largest granite island in the Seychelles. Between Mahé, the main island (45 km/28 mi away) and Praslin there are numerous daily flights (time 15–20 min). There are also fast ferries that take about an hour to make the crossing.

After Mahé, Praslin is the most popular destination for visitors to the Seychelles. The island has a unique charm and a very peaceful atmosphere and offers a wide selection of accommodation in several resorts and hotels (both large and small) that all blend in beautifully and harmoniously with the surrounding landscape. In the past the socialist government had restrictive policies that focused on the high-end of the accommodation market but these policies have been transformed in recent years. The state now not

ISLAND ROUND TRIP

By local standards Praslin has a rather good road network but tourists need to exercise caution as the driving conditions include left-hand drive, narrow roads and the lack of road shoulders. The roadside often drops a few

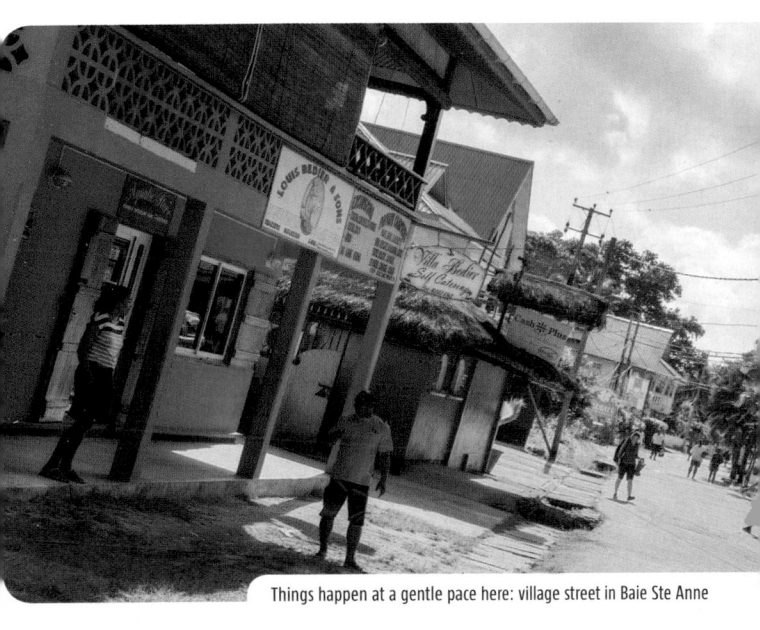

Things happen at a gentle pace here: village street in Baie Ste Anne

only approves of, but even promotes, private initiatives offering affordable rooms in guesthouses. Aside from the unique forest of the Vallée de Mai, Praslin also offers some truly beautiful beaches that frequently appear on the lists of the world's most exquisite beaches.

Until the arrival of tourism, the islanders lived from agriculture and fishing. Both still play a vital role, but nowadays the growing tourism industry provides employment for about half of Praslin's 7,000 inhabitants.

feet straight down so drivers often veer off the road when swerving or trying to overtake!

A good starting point for a round trip is the pier at the Baie Ste Anne, where the ferries leave for Mahé. If you take the road leading into the island interior, you will reach the area of the *Vallée de Mai* National Park after only a few miles. You drive a further 3 km/1.9 mi through an untouched landscape with towering mahogany and eucalyptus trees before you reach the entrance to the park.

Huge palm trees in the
Vallée de Mai National Park

ANSE LAZIO ★
(132 B2) (*M4*)

In the north of Praslin is Anse Lazio, a beach with powdery white sand, sparkling turquoise water and fringed with palm trees and dense lush vegetation. It is without a doubt the most beautiful beach on the island – and ideal for swimming and snorkeling –the word has spread and the beach is now very popular. Nonetheless you can still enjoy the views of the smooth, red granite rocks in crystal clear water. During the northwest monsoon the waves are several feet high.

ANSE POSSESSION
(132 C3) (*N5*)

From Baie Ste Anne the route continues along the coast via Anse Volbert to Anse Possession. It was here that Marion Dufresne erected the so-called *Pierre de Possession* (Possession Stone) in 1768. With this act – also done by Captain Nicolas Morphey on Mahé in 1756 – Dufresne declared the island a French possession and gave the island its current name. The island was named after the minister of the navy at the time, Gabriel de Choiseul, the Duke of Praslin. The island, which you can see from Anse Possession, is called Curieuse. From here the road continues via Anse Boudin to Anse Lazio.

GRAND' ANSE
(132 C4) (*N6*)

The road that runs west from the Vallée de Mai takes you to the southern end of Grand' Anse, where the sea can be quite rough. It offers little in the way of scenic attractions, so it is better to continue along the coast towards the north, to Ste Marie's Point. From the crop of granite boulders, which you will reach after a short walk, you will have a wonderful view of the island and sea.

BLACK PEARL LTD.
(132 B3–4) (*M6*)

Opposite the Praslin Airport you can visit a pearl breeding centre – the only pearl farm in the Indian Ocean – where black pearls are cultivated. However, don't expect too much – sometimes a film demonstrates how the pearls are cultivated. In the shop you can also purchase pearl jewellery; however, it is even more expensive than in the jewellery shops in Victoria. *Mon–Fri 9am–4pm, Sat 9am–midday | admission approx. 38 rupees*

VALLÉE DE MAI NATIONAL PARK ★ ●
(133 D4) (*O6*)

The best way to explore this idyllic World Heritage Site is by hiking the well maintained network of nature trails that run through the valley with its lush canopy of leaves. It is not permitted to leave the signposted pathways. Shortly after the entrance you can see a group of coco de mer palm trees that are estimated to be 800–1,000 years old, almost certainly the oldest specimens of this botanical rarity. It is believed that there are about 6,000 of these palm trees here. Naturally there aren't only coco de mer palms; botanists have counted 43 different species – including all the palm species of the Seychelles and six endemic ones.

With a little luck you may see the rare Black Parrot or small lizards that populate the Vallée de Mai. A hike through the Vallée de Mai should take about 2–3 hours. The paths are designed and signposted in such a way that you can always turn back and return to the starting point. Along the main path is one that branches off and leads to a covered ✂ viewpoint overlooking the valley. *Daily 8am–5.30pm | admission approx. 300 rupees (cash only)*

FOOD & DRINK

BONBON PLUME (132 B2) (*M4*)

Tourists and well off locals alike appreciate the excellent Creole cuisine served in this restaurant right on Anse Lazio. *Daily 12.30pm–3pm, dinner only on request and with a minimum of 10 | Anse Lazio | tel. 423 2136 | Moderate*

BRITANNIA (132 C4) (*N6*)

This is a good option for a break during the island round trip; the excellent Creole cuisine is worth a stop. *Daily | Grand' Anse | tel. 423 3215 | Moderate*

INSIDER TIP ▶ CAPRICORN (132 A3) (*L5*)

Even though the restaurant is a bit out of the way, the trip is well worth it for its widely praised, tasty and affordable local cuisine and delicious sorbets made from local fruits. *Mon–Sat 8am–11pm | Anse Kerlan | tel. 423 3224 | Budget–Moderate*

LE CHÂTEAU DE FEUILLES ✂
(133 E5) (*P7*)

The exclusive hotel's restaurant serves excellent French and Creole cuisine; a

LOW BUDGET

On Praslin it is a real pleasure to take a stroll on *Côte d'Or at Anse Volbert* in the evening when the temperature is perfect. On the way there are a few street restaurants with reasonably priced local specialities.

Right opposite the jetty on La Digue is a supermarket where you can purchase Seychelles spice mixtures at affordable prices. The cooking instructions are sometimes quite funny…

speciality of the house is the grilled crayfish (a freshwater lobster) with garlic butter. Make your reservation well in advance! Unique views of the islands offshore of Praslin. *Daily, only evenings | Pointe Cabris | tel. 429 00 00 | Expensive*

LEISURE & SPORTS

HIKING

One particularly lovely hike leads from *Ste Marie's Point* to *Anse Lazio,* one of the most beautiful beaches in the Seychelles. However, some of the paths are not maintained and are difficult to follow. Ask the locals for the way. The hike begins at the bus station at *Ste Marie's Point,* buses leave there for *Grand' Anse.* Below the path, which leads through a lush landscape in a northerly direction, you will see the Anse Kerlan River. On the bank to the north is a bridge over the river along a range of hills, and further on a steep pathway that leads down to *Anse Lazio.*

ENTERTAINMENT

There is a party atmosphere on Fri/Sat from 10pm at *Oxygen Nightclub* at Baie Ste Anne *(tel. 423 29 62)*, they have a dress code so make sure you are wearing something elegant. In some hotels and at the *Coco Bello* bands perform on Saturdays. Another hotspot is the *Jungle Club (tel. 451 26 83)*, which is open on Fridays and Saturdays from 10pm: their motto is 'As wild as it gets'.

WHERE TO STAY

BEACH VILLA ☆
(132 C4) (*Ω N6*)

Small hotel with family atmosphere, the accommodation is in chalets right on the beach. Nine rooms with wonderful views of the neighbouring is-

lands of Cousin and Cousine. The hotel organises boat trips to other islands, as well as deep sea fishing and snorkelling. *Grand' Anse | tel. 423 34 45 | martin@seychelles.net | Budget*

BERJAYA PRASLIN BEACH
(133 D3) (*Ω O5*)

While this is not a five star hotel it is very popular due to its relaxed, friendly atmosphere. The 79 lovely rooms offer garden, sea and swimming pool views. Restaurant, three bars and a large swimming pool. Windsurfing, snorkelling and deep sea fishing are on offer. *Anse Volbert | tel. 428 62 86 | www.berjayahotel.com/praslin | Budget–Moderate*

HOTEL CAFÉ DES ARTS
(133 D3) (*Ω O5*)

This mini hotel – it has just five rooms – is so pleasant and popular that you have to book early. Both the location, right on the beach, and the tastefully designed décor of the establishment are exceptional. It belonged to the artist Christine Harter and you can view her INSIDER TIP works and those by other artist in the small gallery. The spacious rooms have bathrooms with outdoor showers. There is also a small restaurant (lunch and dinner) that serves top quality seafood and decadent desserts. *Anse Volbert | tel. 423 21 70 | www.cafe.sc | Moderate–Expensive*

LE CHÂTEAU DE FEUILLES
(133 E5) (*Ω P7*)

Not far from the ferry pier lies this beautiful, but relatively expensive hotel, with just nine luxurious suites. The hotel is surrounded by a large park, there is a swimming pool overlooking the sea and on weekends guests can take a boat trip to the private island of *Grande Sœur* which belongs to the hotel. *Pointe*

Cabris | tel. 429 00 00 | www.chateaude feuilles.com | Expensive

CHAUVE SOURIS ISLAND LODGE
(133 D3) *(Ø O5)*

At first glance one wouldn't suspect that there is a hotel on the tiny granite island off Côte d'Or. Surrounded by some mas-

able, tastefully furnished �►☰ **INSIDER TIP** *Black Parrot Suites* on a hill. There are fantastic views from their terraces! ● Wonderful massages with individually mixed oils. Point of departure for boat trips, jetty and tennis court. *Anse Bois de Rose | tel. 429 05 55 | www.cocodemer. com | Expensive*

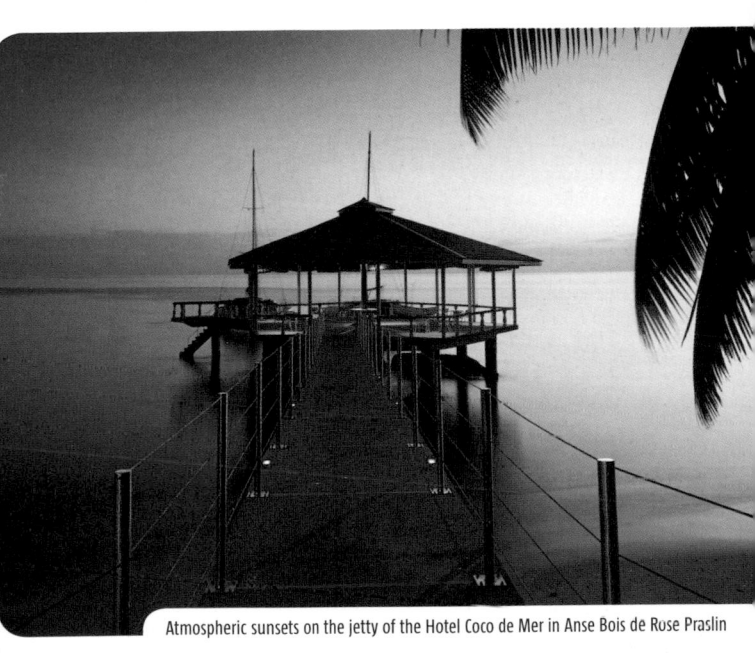

Atmospheric sunsets on the jetty of the Hotel Coco de Mer in Anse Bois de Rose Praslin

sive trees and lush vegetation is a villa (with only five rooms) and a bungalow. The boutique hotel offers all the comforts with an all-inclusive package. Minimum stay is three days. All water sports available. *Chauve Souris Island | tel. 423 22 00 | Expensive*

COCO DE MER
(133 D5) *(Ø O7)*

The 52 spacious bungalows are set in a beautiful tropical garden bordering the sea. Particularly inviting are the comfort-

COLIBRI GUESTHOUSE ☼
(133 E5) *(Ø P7)*

A family run guesthouse with great view over the Ste Anne Bay, with 12 rooms. Diving excursions can be organised on request. *Pointe Cabris | tel. 429 42 00 | www.colibrisweethome.com | Budget–Moderate*

CONSTANCE LÉMURIA RESORT
(132 A2) *(Ø L5)*

Five star luxury hotel in a picturesque location on one of the most beautiful beaches in Praslin. Tasteful décor and particularly attractive suites. Restaurant serving Creole and international cuisine, spa and fitness centre, ● 18 hole golf course (the only one on the Seychelles). *104 rooms | Anse Kerlan | tel. 428 12 81 | www.lemuriaresort. com | Expensive*

INDIAN OCEAN LODGE ⚓
(132 B–C4) (ω N6)

Well maintained, spacious hotel complex on Grand' Anse with a magnificent garden. There are 32 very comfortable rooms in eight separate units. On the beach there is a highly acclaimed restaurant serving Creole and international cuisine. There are daily excursions to the neighbouring nature conservation islands of Cousin, Aride and Curieuse. *Grand' Anse | tel. 428 38 38 | www.indi anoceanlodge.com | Moderate*

RAFFLES PRASLIN SEYCHELLES
(133 D5) (ω O7)

This luxury hostel was opened in 2011 and is part of the same hotel group as the legendary *Raffles* in Singapore. All of the modern villas have private swimming pools and views of Anse Takamaka and Curieuse Island. Restaurants, bars and perfect service all meet the legendarily high standards of the group. The spa has 13 treatment rooms offering all the therapies designed to uplift, soothe and restore your wellbeing. Numerous water sports and excursion trips on offer. *86 villas | Anse Takamaka | tel. 429 60 00 | www.raffles.com/ praslin | Expensive*

LA RÉSERVE
(133 D3) (ω O5)

Quiet hotel that is well suited to families due to its spacious and manicured gardens, but it is not cheap. The rooms are spread over several buildings, in front is Anse Petite Cour, a long private beach with many water sport activities. The Jetty restaurant is unique: it looks like a ship's pier, but has never been used as one. At least once a week there is an excellent Creole buffet that is open to both hotel guests and visitors. Book in advance and dress appropriately! *40 rooms | Anse Petite Cour | tel. 429 80 00 | www.lareserve.sc | Expensive*

VILLAS DE VOYAGEUR
(132 A3) (ω L5)

There are only two rooms in this lovely guesthouse at the end of Anse Kerlan, which you can see from the private terrace. Or you can sit in the beautifully landscaped garden and watch the sunset. They are fully equipped for self-catering and there are also shops nearby. On request the owner herself will create a special Creole meal. *2 rooms | Anse Kerlan | tel. 423 31 61 | www.villas duvoyageur.sc | Budget*

ISLANDS IN THE VICINITY

CURIEUSE
(132–133 C–D 1–2) (ω N–O4)

Just over a mile from Praslin is the tiny (1 mi²) island of Curieuse, which received its name in 1768 from one of the ships on the expedition led by Marion Dufresne. The island is part of the Marine National Park and cannot be developed. It was once a leper colony, today only the warden and his family live here with about 250 giant tortoises. There are also numerous nesting places for the protected hawksbill turtles. Divers and snorkellers can find fantastic places in the coral garden at Pointe Rouge. Daily trips to Curieuse are offered by almost all the hotels on Praslin.

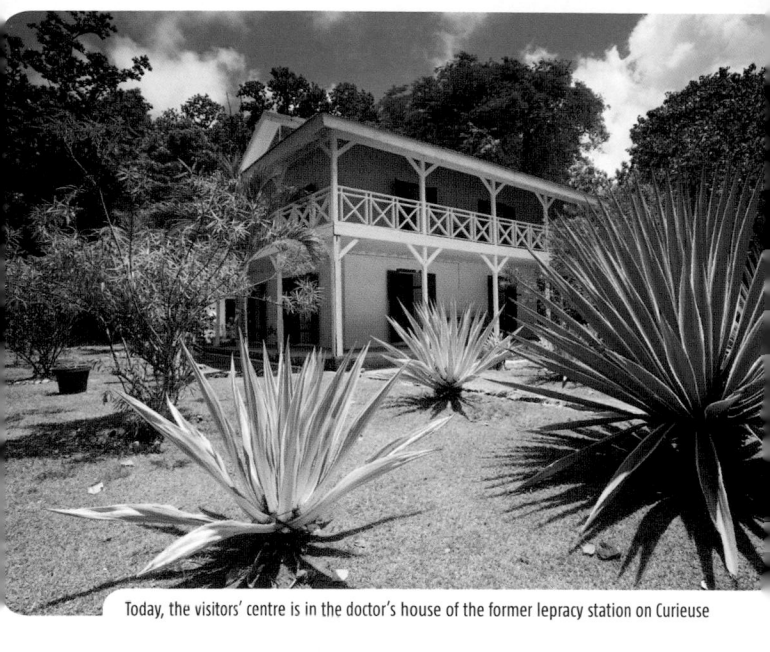

Today, the visitors' centre is in the doctor's house of the former lepracy station on Curieuse

The house on Curieuse was built in 1870 and served as home to the leper colony doctor. For the last few years the building has housed an *Eco Museum* and a *Visitor Centre (daily 8am–5pm | admission approx. 150 rupees)*.

ROUND ISLAND (133 F4) (*Ⓜ Q6–7*)

Round Island (not to be confused with the eponymous island off Mahé) in front of the wide bay on Praslin's east side offers INSIDER TIP fantastic diving and snorkelling opportunities. Baie Ste Anne is only about 5 km/3.1 mi away and there are daily trips to the island from there.

DAY TRIPS

Operators on Praslin offer half day or full day trips to several neighbouring islands. On Cousin in the south-west and on Curieuse in the north, the pristine nature is the main attraction, and off St Pierre you can cool down at the end of the day by going snorkelling. Visitors are taken to the islands by boat and are then accompanied by guides on hikes across the islands. And the guides will gladly answer any questions you have. The hikes are not strenuous and the inclines gentle but you should still take plenty of water, sun block and insect repellent. Meals on the beach are included. The experience is unique, but not cheap *(approx. 1,550 rupees)*. The landing fees that are on each island are one of the reasons for the steep price. But as these revenues benefit conservation, you should rather consider the fee a donation. There are a number of companies that offer the service so it is best to make enquiries at your hotel reception. Participants are collected by bus from the hotel.

BIRD ISLAND & DENIS ISLAND

You need both a deep wallet and a bit of luck to visit the two sister islands of Bird and Denis. The word is out that these two coral islands (just 50 km/31.1 mi apart from each other) are two of the great natural treasures of the Seychelles.
As the accommodation is limited the islands are often quickly booked up and many tourists don't get to see them, which is a real pity. Yet again it may not be so bad because this means that there is a good chance that the islands remain what they are meant to be in the first place: a retreat. Not merely for work-weary holidaymakers but also for the flora and fauna.

Whilst the largest part of the Seychelles consists of granite, Bird and Denis Islands are coral islands. Their seabed foundation is also granite but over centuries – per-

haps even thousands of years – colourful corals have grown over it in all their splendour. A lot of sunlight, warm, clean water with plenty of plankton and constant sea currents are the ideal conditions for the growth of corals. Protecting them should be a given. Unfortunately, over-exploitation has taken place over the past decades, not only underwater, but on the islands themselves. One example was the wholesale exploitation of guano, which was once used all over the world as a fertiliser. Up to 1905 a massive 17,000 tons of it was exported to Mauritius to fertilize the sugar cane fields. Today there is so little demand for guano, due to the availability of chemical fertilisers, that its removal can no longer be justified. Something that has had a positive effect on the nature as the

Visiting Esmeralda and friends – seabirds, colourful corals and fantastic island landscapes straight out of a travel brochure

flora and fauna have once again found an ecological balance.

BIRD ISLAND (ÎLE AUX VACHES)

(0) *(M–N1)* 'Is ★ Esmeralda still alive?' This is a question that the owner of Bird Island (also Île aux Vaches),

approx. 100 km/62 mi north of Mahé, has to answer quite frequently. And not without reason.

After all, this tortoise, with the rather misleading– for a male – name of Esmeralda is believed to be over 170 years old. Some sources even say it is 200 years old – but that is obviously difficult to prove. He is approx. 300 kg/660 lbs and 1.80 m/5.9 ft long and is the oldest known giant tortoise in the world. Esmeralda is undoubtedly the most prominent resident of Bird

BIRD ISLAND (ÎLE AUX VACHES)

Island. The small island (1.5 km/0.9 mi long and 600 m/1,968 ft wide) was first known as Île aux Vaches (island of the dugongs) after the numerous sea cows that once lived in these waters.

This northernmost island of the Seychelles was discovered in 1756 by the Irish Captain Nicolas Morphey, who sailed to the Seychelles and annexed a whole series of islands for France at

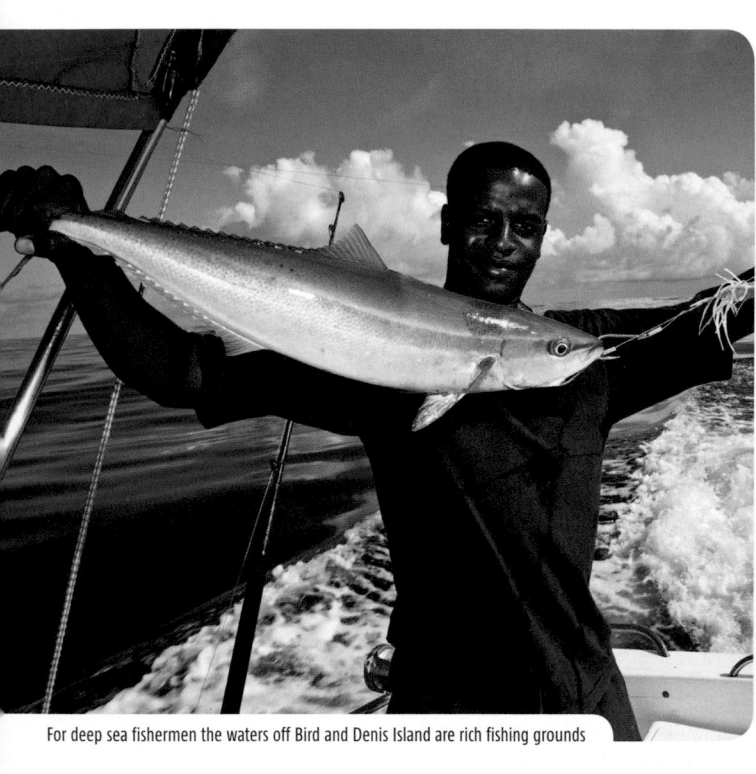

For deep sea fishermen the waters off Bird and Denis Island are rich fishing grounds

Besides the tortoises, who are permanent residents of the island, two other species of marine turtles use Bird Island to lay their eggs: the hawksbill turtle and the green turtle. Because the Seychelles are the only place where these turtles can also lay their eggs during the day, there is no better place to observe them than here. Of course you need to be very careful, and follow all the rules so that you do not interfere with this unique natural spectacle.

the behest of King Louis XV. Today Bird Island is privately owned and the owner certainly knows what he is doing. The 24 bungalows are often fully booked – a consequence of the company's philosophy that states you may only visit the island if you sleep over at least one night. Bird Island is a coral island on the edge of the Mahé Plateau, not far from the edge of the island the plateau drops off to a depth of more than 1,800 m/5,900 ft. The island owes its tropical vegetation to the rich guano deposited by the tens of thousands of terns that regularly return here to breed. The resulting fertile soil is rich in organic compounds so not only do coconut trees flourish here but also mangos, papayas and avocados.

SIGHTSEEING

BIRD SANCTUARY ★

The northeastern part of the island is a bird sanctuary, and this is what makes the island such an attraction. You can view the birds from an ☗ observation deck – however, entering the protected area itself is not allowed. The most interesting time to visit is in the late afternoon or in the early evening when INSIDER TIP ▸ millions of Sooty Terns return from their daily forage for food at sea. Their excited chatter and clamour sounds for all the world as though they are regaling their companions with the adventures of their day – that is the impression anyway! The Sooty Terns only require dry land from April to October, when they raise their young – they spend the rest of the year (at least according to the ornithologists) flying across the ocean. They sleep on the water at night.

Besides Esmeralda there is a second giant tortoise on Bird Island (and about 40 human inhabitants). Both tortoises do not come from here though, they were brought here a long time ago from the far distant Aldabra Atoll.

FOOD & DRINK/ WHERE TO STAY

BIRD ISLAND LODGE

The lodge's palm-thatched bungalows have spacious and attractively furnished rooms, with small terraces overlooking the sea. Delicious Creole meals are served in the restaurant. *24 bungalows | information and bookings (only full packages) in Victoria on Mahé: P. O. Box 1419 | tel. 422 49 25 | www.birdislandseychelles. com | Expensive*

LEISURE & SPORTS

As long as you don't disturb the birds, you are given free rein to enjoy yourself at leisure. The hotel owner offers guests a motorboat for deep sea fishing excursions and there is excellent snorkelling in the clear waters off the southern part of the island at high tide.

ENTERTAINMENT

Don't expect exciting evening entertainment on this peaceful island. A good book, a bottle of wine and some stimulating conversation with other island guests is ample compensation for any lack of nightclubs and bars.

★ **Esmeralda**
A celebrity giant tortoise that has legendary status for being at least 170 years old → **p. 69**

★ **Bird sanctuary**
Take a guided tour of the northeast of Bird Island – ornithology included → **p. 71**

★ **Denis Island round trip**
Through the dense forest to an old lighthouse → **p. 72**

★ **House reef off Denis**
Not far from the shore a reef with a 30 m/98.4 ft drop – exciting for divers → **p. 73**

MARCO POLO HIGHLIGHTS

DENIS ISLAND

(0) *(🗺 O–P1)* **Denis Island is as flat as a pancake and a mere 0.5 mi² and from here it is only about another 8 km/5 mi to the area of the seabed where the coastal Mahé Plateau drops down 1,800 m/5,900 ft.**

The island only rises about 3.5 m/11.5 ft out of the sea and is completely surrounded by a protective coral reef – a **INSIDER TIP** fantastic area for snorkellers and divers. In contrast to most of the other islands, which rise from the underwater granite plateau, Denis is a genuine coral island that came into existence a lot later than for example La Digue, Praslin or the main island of Mahé. Denis is privately owned, and that is also the reason why you can only book a flight to the island when you have made a reservation to stay overnight. Exclusivity is the trump card here – and this is reflected in the steep room rates of about 13,800 rupees per night.

There is also an interesting myth that a pirate's treasure has lain hidden for centuries somewhere on Denis Island. Several treasure hunts here – and on other islands – have thus far all been unsuccessful. However, the skeleton of a man (whose identity is still a mystery) was discovered.

You can either reach the island with the supply boat that travels regularly between Mahé and Denis, or conveniently, with the plane that operates daily. Full packages are available at the travel agencies in Victoria on Mahé. The flight only takes half an hour.

SIGHTSEEING

ROUND TRIP ★

Denis Island is almost completely covered by a dense forest of Kasuarina and Takamaka trees and coconut palms. You shouldn't expect any special botanical rarities or anything sensational during a trip around the island,

CHARTER BOATS

It is well worth chartering a boat if you want to go fishing or diving. You can get information from several operators. The main providers are *VPM* and *Sunsail*. The central contact point on the Seychelles is the *Marine Charter Association (P.O. Box 204 | Victoria, Mahé | tel. 422 46 79 | mca@seychelles.net)*.

You can explore the Seychelles archipelago on your own with a sailing or motor yacht, a great alternative to a hotel room holiday. Day or weekly charters are available at Azur Yachting Seychelles on Eden Island *(tel. 424 25 16 or 271 91 21 | www. azuryachtingseychelles.com)*; also on Eden Island is the international charter operator *Moorings* (www. moorings.com) they offer a bareboat cruise but skippers with experience of the area can also be organised. Luxury catamarans with full crew are available from *Elegant Yachting (Eden Island | tel. 451 57 36 | www.elegant-yachting.com)*.

which should only take you about an hour and a half at a leisurely pace. But you can observe a few giant tortoises and, if you have a keen eye, you may also spot a few pretty, colourful tropical birds in the trees. At the northern tip of the island is a lighthouse dating to the turn of the century and two deserted stone buildings that once probably served as a prison.

FOOD & DRINK/ WHERE TO STAY

DENIS ISLAND LODGE
The 25 bungalow resort offers all the creature comforts and is located on the west coast of the island, near the airstrip. The only restaurant is operated by the hotel. The cuisine served is delicious as almost all the ingredients are grown on the island itself and are therefore always wonderfully fresh. *Reservations (Victoria) 428 89 63 | www.denis island.com | Expensive*

LEISURE & SPORTS

Denis Island is surrounded by fine but rather narrow sandy beaches. The island's real attraction is underwater off the western coast: not far from the shore is the ★ Denis house reef where, at depths of up to 30 m/98.4 ft, you can find an extraordinary variety of sea creatures. The area around the island is teeming with fish. Interestingly the damages that were caused by the global climate phenomenon of El Niño in 1998 are only visible in exposed areas. Although renowned marine biologists predicted that it would take many years for the corals to recover from the sudden flow of warm water, many of the soft corals are growing back.

Bird's-eye perspective of Denis Island

In terms of sports activities, there are sailing boats, surfboards and fishing equipment on offer.

ENTERTAINMENT

All the trials and tribulations of your everyday life will melt away when you enjoy a spectacular Seychelles sunset. Nightlife? Forget it!

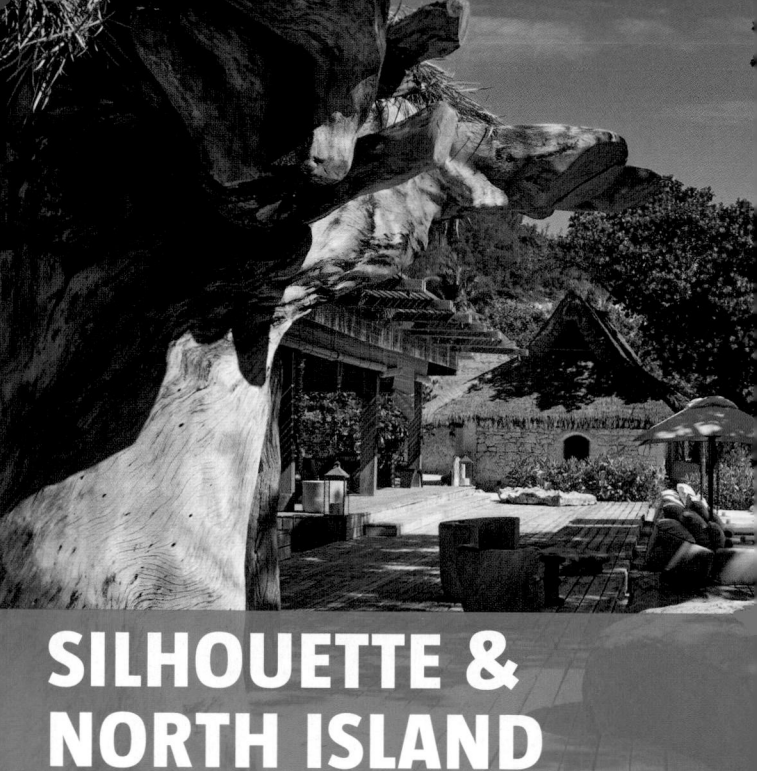

SILHOUETTE & NORTH ISLAND

No matter whether you only do a day trip or if you choose this lush and mountainous island (7 mi²) as your holiday home: a visit to Silhouette Island, off the north-west coast of Mahé, is a holiday must.

This is probably how Mahé looked before man arrived and intervened in nature: it is characterised by dense rain forest and lush, tropical flora that gives it a similar feel to Mahé, and features three mountains with a height of more than 500 m/1,640 ft. At a height of 751 m/2,464 ft ⚡ **INSIDER TIP** Mount Dauban is the third highest mountain in the Seychelles. A strenuous hike to the summit of the mountain will be rewarded with some dramatic scenery and a wonderful view of Mahé.

The fauna is just as diverse as the flora and in addition to several dozen giant tortoises there are the countless bird species, which you can see when you do your leisurely trip around the island. Silhouette is only 18 km/11.2 mi away from Mahé, consisting of pure granite and is the third largest island of the Inner Islands. There is no airport on the island as the landscape is too mountainous and it is very close to the main island of Mahé. It is more complicated to get to the North Island. The unspoilt, tropical island is private property and can only be visited with permission or as holiday accommodation. Aimed at well heeled guests, it is one of the world's most expensive retreats (approx. 46,000 rupees per person/night) and ensures total lux-

The islands are popular with hikers: dense rain forest, tropical vegetation and pristine beaches in exclusive seclusion

ury, privacy and exclusivity for its clientele. North Island is located 6 km/3.7 mi from Silhouette and 25 km/15.5 mi from Mahé (transfer by helicopter).

SILHOUETTE

(136 A–C 1–3) (∅ A–C 5–7) The island is named after the French Finance Minister, Etienne de Silhouette, who apparently decorated his house with (cheap) silhouettes instead of (expensive) paintings and in so doing also gave this silhouette its name.

Europeans first discovered the island in 1767 but there were probably Arab seafarers on the island several centuries before. The island's history is inextricably linked with the history of the Dauban family, who immigrated to the Seychelles from France in the mid-19th century. Auguste Dauban became wealthy through the trade with copra and coconut plantations and bought the island of Silhouette. Around 1860 he constructed a

SILHOUETTE

Since the mid-19th century, coconuts have been cultivated on Silhouette

wonderful house made of Takamaka wood which was called *Grande Case* by the island locals. It was furnished with exquisite furniture, and they ate from the finest Chinese porcelain. The Dau-ban family line has died out but one of the last in the dynasty line participated as javelin thrower at the Olympic Games in Paris in 1924 thanks to the skills he acquired as a child harpooning for fish in the reefs of Silhouette.

Today there are three small villages with about 200 inhabitants, who live mainly from the coconut harvest. They produce copra from the coconut flesh. They also cultivate spice plants, coffee, tobacco and tropical fruits. Since the construction of the luxury hotel, the *Hilton Labriz*, new jobs have also been created in tourism. The island itself is – besides the parts around the harbour – not easily accessible and therefore serves as a home for many rare plants. Even though the villages are all along the coast, it is often not possible to reach them by boat across the water due to rough swell. Therefore the only choice for residents and visitors is to take the rather arduous route through the forest. Silhouette can easily be reached via the channel (rich in fish) that separates the island from Mahé. Boat owners at Beau Vallon Beach of-fer day trips and also have fishing equip-ment on board (so lunch is assured). The passage takes about an hour.

SIGHTSEEING

ROUND TRIP ★

You should plan on at least half a day for an island round trip. It is best to em-ploy a guide (at the harbour) who can lead the way as the route is sometimes steep and the paths confusing. As com-pensation for the somewhat strenuous hike you will get to experience an im-pressive and largely unspoilt landscape with a rich variety of plants and animals. One such botanical rarity is a carnivorous INSIDER TIP▶ pitcher plant that is endemic to the island; there are several beautiful specimens on Silhouette.

ANSE MONDON ●
(134 A– B1) (*Ⓜ B5*)

Anse Mondon on the north side of Sil-houette is *the* picture-perfect beach, one that is well known from postcards. However, you need to bank on about a two hour walk to get there and in plac-es the path leads over smooth rocks, so it is best not to set out when it is raining. You will be rewarded with one of the most beautiful beaches in the Seychelles. Remember to take your mask and snorkel so you can also explore its fascinating underwater world.

ARAB GRAVES ★
(134 C3) (*∅ C6*)

Thirty graves at the *Anse Lascars* are silent witnesses to the fact that Arab seafarers arrived on the island from about the 9th century. You can combine a visit to the graves with a very interesting hike through the lush, overgrown nature. Just follow the path that starts left of the harbour; it leads along the coast and ends abruptly at a high rocky reef. A short walk from the harbour is the INSIDER TIP Dauban family tomb and mausoleum. A marble plaque at the entrance bears the inscription, 'Dying is not dying, my friends, dying is just change...' On the way you will undoubtedly come across a few giant tortoises and – if you pay careful attention – you may also see a few tropical birds in the forests below Mont Gratte Fesse.

LA PASSE
(134 C2) (*∅ C5*)

If you come by boat from Mahé, the small village of La Passe is the first port of call on the east coast of Silhouette. Opposite is an old house that is one of the most beautiful old style colonial houses in the Seychelles, the houses of La Passe are to the right.

FOOD & DRINK/ WHERE TO STAY

LA BELLE TORTUE
(134 C2) (*∅ C5*)

The *La Belle Tortue* also places a lot of emphasis on exclusivity and privacy.

In the lodge there are nine remarkably plush rooms and lodges, as well as a restaurant right on the beach, a bar, a spa and a dive school nearby that runs PADI courses. There are daily excursions for divers and snorkellers. *Tel. 432 53 35 | www.labelletortue.com | Moderate–Expensive*

HILTON SEYCHELLES LABRIZ RESORT & SPA ★ (134 C1–2) (*∅ C5*)

The only hotel on Silhouette Island also happens to be one of the finest establishments that can be booked in the Seychelles. Along the mile long, sandy beach of Anse La Passe are 111 chalets, the smallest almost 1,000 ft², the largest nearly 2,000 ft², all with their own private garden and swimming pool. Everything you expect of a five star resort is on offer here. Pamper yourself with spa treatments in the wellness centre, exert yourself with one of the many water sports or join a guided nature walk.

MARCO POLO HIGHLIGHTS

★ **Arab graves**
Inscriptions may be hard to decipher – but the Arabs really were there → p. 77

★ **Silhouette Island round trip**
Visit an indigenous carnivorous plant → p. 76

★ **Hilton Seychelles Labriz Resort & Spa**
The only hotel on Silhouette, but a superb one! → p. 77

★ **North Island Resort**
Kate and William spent their honeymoon here – when are you coming? → p. 79

The on site dive centre regularly organises trips out to pristine underwater dive spots. There are no less than five top class restaurants that offer culinary delights from all around the world. *Reservations in Victoria: tel. 429 39 49 | www. seychelleslabriz.hilton.com | Expensive*

NORTH ISLAND

(0) (⟐ B–C1) A remarkable feature of this small (500 acres) densely verdant island are its three magnificent granite 'mountains'. They reach a height of 214 m/702 ft above sea level. North Island – Île du Nord in French – is ideal for walking and hiking.

In 1609 North Island was the first granite island in the Seychelles to be explored by Europeans, but this first – British – expedition was without consequence. Thereafter the coves and caves along the coast became the ideal hideouts for pirates on the lam. On a trip around the world the well heeled British amateur botanical artist, Marianne North, stopped off here and her impressive Seychelles paintings can still be admired in England to this day.

The first settlers on North Island made their living from the cultivation and processing of coconuts and other fruits. When the coconut industry lost its importance at the end of the 19th century, they left the island. The island became overgrown with weeds and infested with rats and vermin. Even the indigenous wildlife nearly died out. Then in the mid 1990s it was rediscovered by a private investment group from South Africa who decided to not only make the island a haven for well-heeled guests, but also to start a remarkable nature conservation project. The initiative meant that the natural habitat has been fully restored and there are now many indigenous animals, especially birds, who have once again settled here. ⊙ The management also wants to make North Island energy-neutral by means of solar power and the collection of rainwater – on a rainy day as much as 30,000 litres of water can be collected.

North Island is one of the most fertile islands in the whole archipelago. Only a

SEYCHELLES COMPACT

Each island in the Seychelles has its own charms, and you shouldn't limit your visit to only one of them. The best option is to do some island hopping in the Inner Islands and there are various organisations available to you. The ships are not the large ocean liners, but agile sailing boats such as the 'Sea Shell', the 'Sea Bird' or the 'Sea Star'. They take a maximum of 16 passengers and also stop along the way to give you the opportunity to have a swim or go for a dive. Accommodation and full board are included, and a number of islands are visited and separate trips to them would otherwise have cost a lot more money. The bottom line is that these cruises are a fairly inexpensive alternative to a hotel vacation. The ideal option is to combine both. *Information: www.seychelles-cruises. com* few years ago almost 100 residents still lived from vegetable cultivation, livestock and fishing. Until the opening of the new North Island Resort (2003) there was no place for tourists to stay overnight.

ment places great importance on letting their visitors know about the continuous environmental measures taken to ensure nature conservation despite the fact that they are running a hotel business.

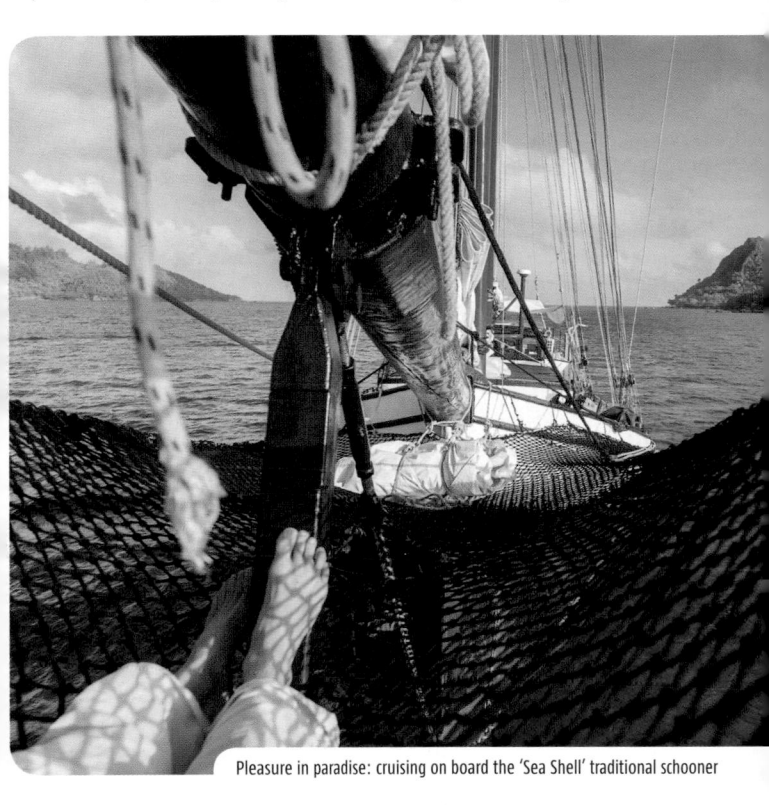

Pleasure in paradise: cruising on board the 'Sea Shell' traditional schooner

WHERE TO STAY

NORTH ISLAND RESORT ★ ☻

Opened in 2003, this five star resort has eleven bungalows and belongs to the category of resorts – similar to the resorts on Frégate and Cousine – that offers its guests the ultimate in luxury in the midst of unspoilt nature. The bungalows are along the flat coast and are shielded from each other. The manage-

The guests receive detailed information and can talk to any of the researchers and the nature conservationists working here. The high price of accommodation (up to 74,800 rupees (!) per person/night) is justified with the argument that a large proportion of the income goes back into the environment and nature conservation. The hotel is marketed by a South African company. *www.north-island.com* | *Expensive*

OUTER SEYCHELLES

The journey is admittedly a little long and difficult but those who venture out will be richly rewarded, because the atolls and islands of the Outer Seychelles create an unusual contrast to what is usually defined as typical of the Seychelles.

These islands do not consist of granite but – just as Denis and Bird Island – they are the product of corals that have been growing for thousands of years. In contrast to the islands of the Inner Seychelles they are not on the underwater Mahé Plateau described in the introduction, but are a good 200 km/124 mi south-west of the main island Mahé.

The islands of the Outer Seychelles are among the finest that the archipelago off the African coast has to offer: beaches with sand like powder, crystal clear water and a fascinating underwater world. It also appears as though nature has recovered faster from the destruction created by the 1998 El Niño climate phenomenon than was predicted.

The Farquhar Group of the Outer Islands has their own flora and fauna world, one that seems rather modest in comparison to the islands rich in species that you find elsewhere on the Seychelles. However, their underwater world is interesting, presenting exceptional diversity, because the Farquhar Group consists primarily of flat coral islands, scattered over a surface area of 40 mi². Coconut palms grow on the islands – such as on Providence Atoll in the northern part of the Farquhar

Photo: Cave diving off Desroches

Coral islands with spectacular beaches and a fascinating underwater world: paradise has a name

Group and on the main island of Providence – and are exploited commercially. Several contract workers also live here, but there is no accommodation for visitors. The journey there is also not easy, as the small island airport is only used for individual charter flights. If you are interested, the best contact is the *Island Development Company (IDC)* in Mahé *(tel. 438 46 40 | idc@seychelles.sc)*.

However, there is another option to get to the Outer Islands and the islands of the Farquhar Group. They are a popular destination for sailing trips, and the local skippers know exactly which islands are allowed to be visited and those that are off limits due to nature conservation restrictions. However, it is very important that you find out the current security situation from the tourism authorities on Mahé (or *www.seychelles.travel*) before undertaking such a trip. In 2010 this remote region was beset by Somalian pirates who seized a tourist boat for ransom and only released it once their high financial demands were met.

ALDABRA ATOLL

(134–135 A–E 4–6) (*A–E 17–18*)

The islands of the Aldabra Atoll are located – far outside of the Mahé Plateau – on a basalt foundation about 1,000 m/3,280 ft deep under the sea.

Giant tortoise on the Aldabra Atoll

The foundation rose upwards about 80,000 years ago, presumably through a volcanic eruption – and sank again leaving the edge of the crater.

There are only 20 residents on the 14 islands that form the atoll: Grande Terre, Île Dubois, Îles aux Cèdres, Îlot Emile, Île Esprit, Îlot Lanier, Îlot Magnan, Île Moustiques, Îlot Parc, Île Michel, Malabar, Picard, Polymnie and Îlot Yangue.

The largest islands are Grande Terre (South Island) and Malabar (Middle Island); altogether the Aldabra group comprises a land surface area of just 60 mi². The entire island of Mahé could fit into the lagoon. If you combined the total area of land and lagoon, the Aldabra Atoll would be the largest in the Indian Ocean with 140 mi².

Hard to believe and yet true: if it were up to British strategists, today there would be a military base in the Aldabra Atoll. However, this did not come to pass thanks to the Labour cabinet in London that campaigned in 1971 to surrender any military presence east of the Suez Canal. And so the Aldabra Atoll was spared that fate.

The isolation of the atoll is probably the most significant reason for the preservation of its unique flora and fauna. Aldabra was already known to Arab seafarers in the 9th century as the name *alkhadra* (the green one) suggests. Later, around 1502, the explorer Vasco da Gama visited the Aldabra Atoll for a few days. In more recent history Aldabra was first sighted by Lazare Picault in 1742. Afterwards the island was visited every now and then by ships passing by, but the landing was difficult, the terrain inhospitable, and there was no fresh water. Potential settlers left to continue their journey after a short stay. Only a few Chinese settled here at the beginning of the 20th century to gather the fibres from the sea cucumbers which are considered a delicacy in the Far East. Parts of the mangrove forest were cut down and vast numbers of tortoises and turtles were killed – also for consumption.

The Aldabra Atoll is considered the home of the ★ *giant tortoises.* At the beginning of the 20th century they were close to extinction. Thousands of tortoises landed in soup pots of eccentric gourmets all over the world. The naturalist Charles Darwin was the first to point out the danger of extinction; he saw the animals as living witnesses of a bygone era of earth's history. They are said to have survived 200 million years without any significant change in their appearance.

Today the giant tortoises enjoy strict environmental protection and their population has fortunately recovered once again. On the entire atoll there are now almost 150,000 tortoises while there are also some turtle species that visit as temporary guests when they arrive here to lay their eggs from December to March. Tortoises are omnivores, but their main diet consists of plants and grasses.

The fact that the Aldabra Atoll has been a Unesco protected World Heritage Site since 1976 also means that access is not that easy and requires special permission. This is included if you participate in an organised expedition. You can find out more current information at the tourist office at the Independence House in Victoria on Mahé. This also applies to the current situation regarding the dangers of raids by Somalian pirates on tourist ships and sail-boats. As there are no tourist facilities, you either have to sleep over on the boat or continue your journey on the same day. The trip on the 'Indian Ocean Explorer' costs about US\$ 325/£ 255 a day per person, the charter flight to Assumption US\$ 1,000/£ 785.

If you are given approval to access the islands in the atoll, you will encounter some remarkable nature: INSIDER TIP▶ more than 270 different plants grow here, of which about two dozen are endemic. Botanical specialities such as the Aldabra Lily and the Aldabra Screwpines are quite remarkable. But you have to have a keen eye, because at first glance the flora doesn't appear to be very spectacular and seems limited to mangroves, coconut palms and shrubs. There is also a rich variety of fauna, including dozens of bird species, such as the White-throated Rail, the last flightless bird in the Indian Ocean, or the Aldabra Drongo, a songbird that is found only on the Aldabra Atoll. The diversity of the flora and fauna endemic to the Aldabra Atoll is down to its status as a Unesco World Heritage Site.

The lagoon, fed by four channels from the sea, has a tidal range of up to 3 m/9.8 ft and during low tide the lagoon is almost dry. Then you can see the strange and bizarrely formed ★ *mushroom islands*: limestone slabs that have been eroded by water at the base.

★ Giant tortoises
The Aldabra Atoll is believed to be the true home of these mighty reptiles → p. 83

★ Mushroom islands
The Aldabra Atoll is characterised by mushroom-shaped stone formations → p. 83

★ Underwater world
The hauntingly beautiful underwater world off Desroches → p. 86

★ Desroches Island Lodge
Rest, nature, luxury: leave your cares behind → p. 86

MARCO POLO HIGHLIGHTS

AMIRANTE ISLANDS

(0) (🗺 O) This chain of coral islands forms part of the Outer Islands, which stretch from the interior of the Seychelles out towards the African mainland. The main island of Mahé is situated the closest to the chain; the distance from the Amirante isle closest to Mahé is only 220 km/137 mi.

Several archipelagos fall under the Amirantes and include: Alphonse, D'Arros, Rémire, Boudeuse, Desnœufs, Desroches, Étoile and Marie Louise as well as the island groups of the African Banks, the St Joseph's and Poivre atolls. All the islands in the Amirantes are a paradise for seabirds. On Desnœufs for example there are massive colonies of Sooty Terns and it is INSIDER TIP particularly busy during the breeding season from May to July. Some of the bird's eggs are collected and taken to Mahé as they are considered a delicacy.

The Amirantes are mostly made up of small islands and islets, coral reefs and sandbanks, which collectively have a surface area about 4 mi². They were first discovered by Arab seafarers about 1,000 years ago, the discoveries were probably unplanned when their ships accidentally ran aground in the shallow waters. Later, in 1502, the Portuguese explorer Vasco da Gama gave the island group its current name during his second journey to India. It was also he who had more detailed nautical charts drawn up, with even the small sandbanks marked. The current names of the islands cannot be traced back to Arabic or Portuguese origins as the old names were replaced by French names during the colonial era. In 1814, when England and France signed a peace treaty, the Amirante group of islands became part of the English colony of Mauritius, which also included the Seychelles as a whole. Finally, in 1909, when the colonial era ended, the Amirantes became part of the Seychelles.

ALPHONSE (0) (🗺 O)

The three islands in the Alphonse group extend over about 16 km/9.9 mi. The island group is named in honour of the explorer Chevalier Alphonse de Pontevez; St François, the name of the neighbouring island, was named after St Francis de Sales. The triangular coral Alphonse Island is about 1.2 km/0.7 mi wide and lies at the edge of the lagoon, which is very inviting for a swim and is full of fish and turtles. The island is covered by dense groves of coconut palms. Also interesting are the overgrown sisal and cotton wool plantations that date back to the 19th century. The barrier reef is ideal for snorkelling and Alphonse has also become a paradise for fly-fishing.

The recreational options on Alphonse itself are limited, but the island offers a good point of departure for excursions to the islands of the neighbouring atolls of *Bijoutier* and *St François* (approx. 1,230–1,850 rupees). Snorkelling trips cost about 385 rupees, sundowner cruises are about 770 rupees and fishing trips about 1,100 rupees.

The *Alphonse Island Resort (reservations: P. O. Box 378 | Victoria | Mahé | tel. 437 67 50 | www.alphonse-island.com | Expensive)*, on the edge of the lagoon, is currently the accommodation that is the furthest from the main island on the Seychelles. It offers a total of 30 chalets in two categories (completely renovated in 2012) and has a swimming pool, a tennis court and a wellness cen-

A dream for individualists: a deserted beach on the coral island Alphonse

tre. The water sports centre rents out canoes as well as diving and fishing equipment. At the *Bijoutier* restaurant there is always freshly caught fish on the menu. The regional IDC airline flies from Mahé to the island once a week (flight time about 1 hour), and there are charter flights available on request. Flights can only be booked in conjunction with accommodation.

D'ARROS
(0) (𝄞 0)

D'Arros lies 45 km/28 mi from Desroches and is best reached by boat (there are regular day trips to the island). The island – named after the marine commander Baron D'Arros – is worth a visit mainly for its diverse vegetation that covers an area of just 0.5 mi². Although coconut palms grew here naturally, additional plantations were also laid out for the production of copra. The island was once owned by a nephew of the last Shah of Iran, who stopped commercial use and promoted nature conservation but the island is now a nature reserve owned by the Save Our Seas Foundation. The environment has recovered well and the Wedge-tailed Shearwater (the chicks were considered a delicacy in the Seychelles) are now back from the brink of extinction.

DESROCHES
(0) *(ω 0)*

The largest island of the Amirantes is about 230 km/143 mi from Mahé on an undersea basalt plateau. The island has a landing strip for the small island hopper of the IDC *(several times a week, flight time from Mahé 30 minutes)*. Desroches takes its name from a governor who ruled Mauritius in the 18th century. The island can be visited all year round but divers should limit themselves to the months of the north-west monsoon (Dec–March) as that is when there is clear underwater visibility. However, this is also the time that it is unfortunately not possible dive the steep wall at the outer edge of the lagoon – which drops thousands of feet into the depths of the Indian Ocean – due to extremely dangerous currents.

The sightseeing attractions of Desroches lie in almost equal parts above and below the water. On the island itself is the interesting and varied scenery and off its coast, the fascinating and colourful ★ *underwater world* with a myriad of tropical fish and other marine life. Unfortunately some of the corals are still partly bleached. There are a number of hiking trails on the island, mostly lined with palm trees. A walk under the canopy of trees is ideal for observing the island's interesting INSIDER TIP bird life – in addition to the numerous other bird species, there are also common house sparrows, and no one knows quite how they got here.

The ★ *Desroches Island Lodge (tel. 422 90 03 | www.desroches-island.com | Moderate–Expensive)* is the only accommodation on the island, but offers its guests all the creature comforts (including a satellite telephone). The 20 rooms and 26 villas are located only a few feet from the beautiful, white sandy beach. There is a tennis court available for sporty guests. The only restaurant *(Moderate)* on the island also belongs to the hotel. Their speciality

CREOLE FOR TOURISTS

Of course you don't have to learn to speak Creole before you go on holiday – the staff in most of the hotels and restaurants speak English or French, often an additional foreign language (usually German or Italian). But you will be well prepared with a few Creole phrases. It also shows the locals that you are interested in their country.
Where can I find a restaurant? – *Kote i annan en restoran?*
Food/drinks – *Manze/bwar*
The menu, please – *Meni, silvouple*

A beer, please – *En labyer, silvouple*
A cup of coffee, please – *En Kafe, silvouple*
What kind of fish is that? – *Ki mannyer sa pwason i apele?*
Salt, sugar, bread, butter – *disel, disik, dipen, diber*
How much is it? – *Konbyen sa?*
The bill, please – *Bil, silvouple*
Where is the toilet? – *Kote i annan en kabinen, silvouple?*
My apologies! – *Ekskiz!*
No problem – *Pa dekwa*
Thank you! – *Mersi!*

Peace and quiet in beautiful surroundings: Desroches Island Lodge

are delicious and surprisingly inexpensive fish dishes.

Anyone looking for evening entertainment or even hustle and bustle will not find it in the Amirantes – nor on any of the other remote Seychelles islands. It is a far better idea to bring along one or two good books.

IDC flies to the island once a day from Mahé (the flight takes about 30 minutes), also charter flights by request. Flights can only be booked in conjunction with accommodation.

POIVRE (0) *(0 O)*

Poivre Island is also called the island of spice; it was named after the French governor of Mauritius, Pierre Poivre. He has a place in history because he was the first to introduce and grow spices on the Seychelles. It is purely coincidence that *poivre* is the French word for pepper. Poivre is a rewarding destination throughout the year and there are some particularly appealing sailing cruises on offer (information available from tour operators in Victoria on Mahé).

DISCOVERY TOURS

❶ THE SEYCHELLES AT A GLANCE

START: ❶ Victoria (Mahé)
END: ❶⑤ Anse Patates (La Digue)

Distance:
➡ Land route approx. 90 km/55.9 mi

3 days
Driving time (car)
approx. 2 ½ hours

COSTS: ferries, overnight stays, bicycle, admission and meals approx. 11,500 rupees/person, car hire on Mahé approx. 1,100 rupees
WHAT TO PACK: swim wear, sun screen

IMPORTANT TIPS: ferry from Victoria to Praslin daily, except Sun, ferry timetables at *www.catcocos.com*; please arrive on time and leave enough time to buy tickets! Restaurant **Bravo** on ❹ Eden Island closed Sun

Would you like to explore the places that are unique to this region? Then the Discovery Tours are just the thing for you – they include terrific tips for stops worth making, breathtaking places to visit, selected restaurants and fun activities. It's even easier with the Touring App: download the tour with map and route to your smartphone using the QR Code on pages 2/3 or from the website address in the footer below – and you'll never get lost again even when you're offline.

TOURING APP

→ p. 2/3

Explore the different islands of the Seychelles: start on the main island, Mahé, and from here 'hop' by boat to the neighbouring island: Praslin with the beautiful Vallée de Mai National Park and laid back La Digue with the famous granite rocks.

From 8am in **①** **Victoria** → p. 41 you can start at the **Sir Selwyn Selwyn Clarke Market**. After a stroll through the colourful market, **head west out of town in your hire car from the main crossroads and uphill over the steep and winding St Louis Road. When you have left the pass be-**

DAY 1

① **Victoria**

6 km/3.7 mi

Photo: Sir Selwyn Selwyn Clarke Market in Victoria, Mahé

2 Beau Vallon

---

12 km/7.5 mi

---

3 North East Point

---

9 km/5.6 mi

---

4 Eden Island

3.5 km/2.2 mi

---

5 Victoria

hind you, make the descent into the valley to a bigger crossroads and turn left to **2 Beau Vallon** → p. 33, the most vibrant beach on the Seychelles. Here, you can splash in the sea, enjoy watersports and a snack lunch from one of the beach vendors. **Then, on the same route head back to the main crossroads. Here, continue northwards along the coast road and around Mahé's northern tip as far as 3 North East Point**, where the cliffs and sand merge to an impressive landscape and invite you to take a stroll by the water. **From here, follow the route back to Victoria. Head across town and remain on the main road heading south along the east coast** until you reach the artificially created, trendy **4 Eden Island**, which is connected to the main island by a dam. On Eden Island you can look forward to a delicious creole dinner in the **Bravo** Restaurant *(Mon–Sat 12pm–10pm | Eden House | tel. 4 34 60 20 | Budget)*. **Afterwards, head back to 5 Victoria**: at the Hilltop Boutique Hotel *(11 apartments | Serret Road | St Louis | tel. 2 52 68 70 | hilltop-boutique.tophotelseychelles.com | Budget)* you are guaranteed a peaceful night despite the city-centre location.

DISCOVERY TOURS

Today, in Victoria head for Inter Island Key and take the first ferry to **Praslin** → p. 60. The "Cat Cocos" departs at 7.30am and arrives on Praslin about an hour later. The ⑥ **Jetty** is on the south-eastern part of the island where you collect your hire car and **drive around Baie Ste Anne to ⑦ Vallée de Mai National Park** → p. 63. In this natural palm forest, you can spend the morning enjoying a short hike followed by a brief sightseeing tour: **back to Baie Ste Anne and from here along the north coast via Anse Volbert and Anse Possession to the beach of ⑧ Anse Lazio** → p. 62. You should definitely head for lunch to the beach restaurant **Bonbon Plume** *(daily, lunchtime only | tel. 423 21 36 | Moderate)*. Spend the afternoon at this enchanting bay – the ultimate bathing paradise! To round off the day, **drive back on the coast road to ⑨ Anse Volbert** on the Côte d'Or, the 'gold coast' of Praslin. Here treat yourself to a generous INSIDER**TIP** creole buffet and stay overnight in the Laurier Guesthouse *(14 rooms | tel. 423 22 41 | www.laurier-seychelles.com | Budget–Moderate)*.

At 9am, at the jetty join the daily sailing schooner to **La Digue** → p. 56. The trip takes 30 minutes and you arrive in the small ⑩ **harbour** where you can rent a bicycle. **Cycle southwards heading right and along the coast until you reach the plantation ⑪ L'Union Estate that leads deep into the countryside.** Here, you will encounter giant tortoises and an ox in an old **coconut mill**. **Then, continue until the road ends by the water.** From here, the paths wind across magnificent granite cliffs to the famous ⑫ **Anse Source d'Argent**, where you can relax and swim in the shallow water. **Take the same road back to the harbour** where in the afternoon you can enjoy a drink in the harbourside bar ⑬ **Tarosa** *(Sun–Thu until 9pm, Fri/Sat until late | Budget)*. **Then, cycle back in a northerly direction to a fine dinner. Cycle around the northern tip into the ⑭ Anse Banane** where you can savour rather pricey, but delicious seafood at **Chez Jules** *(tel. 423 42 87 | Moderate)*. An overnight stay is well worth it at ⑮ **Anse Patates** on the northern tip in **Hotel Patatran Village** *(20 rooms/ apartments | tel. 429 43 00 | www.patatranseychelles.com | Moderate)*. Next morning, return the bikes and take the boat via Praslin back to Mahé.

DAY 2

53.5 km/33.2 mi

⑥ Jetty

4.5 km/2.8 mi

⑦ Vallée de Mai National Park

13.5 km/8.4 mi

⑧ Anse Lazio

7 km/4.4 mi

⑨ Anse Volbert

DAY 3

13 km/8.1 mi

⑩ Harbour

2 km/1.2 mi

⑪ L'Union Estate

0.5 km/0.3 mi

⑫ Anse Source d'Argent

12.5 km/7.8 mi

⑬ Tarosa

3.5 km/2.2 mi

⑭ Anse Banane

3 km/1.9 mi

⑮ Anse Patates

ROUND TRIP ON SOUTH MAHÉ ISLAND

2

START: **①** Victoria	
END: **①** Victoria	**1 day**
	Driving time approx.
Distance:	2 hours
65 km/40.4 mi	

COSTS: approx. 770 rupees for the hire car, approx. 150 rupees for petrol, approx. 460 rupees/person for meals
WHAT TO PACK: swim wear, sun screen, drinking water

IMPORTANT TIPS: It is recommended to book head to visit **⑤ Michael Adams's studio**: *tel. 436 10 06* **⑥ Pineapple Studio** and **Anchor Café** in **⑦ Anse à la Mouche** closed Sun

Explore Mahé's unspoilt south with its beautiful countryside! Visit the most magical bays on the Seychelles, buy local products, enjoy a relaxing swim and treat yourself to a creole snack!

① Victoria

16 km/9.9 mi

② Vilaz Artizanal

4 km/2.5 mi

③ Anse Royale

09:00am Leave **①** Victoria → p. 41 and head south (via the airport). The coast road passes the airport at Anse aux Pins. After the main junction for the mountain road to Montagne Posée, head right at the third exit towards the artists' village of **②** Vilaz Artizanal → p. 38. In the small tropical wooden huts you can admire – and also buy – traditional craftsmanship, artisan model ships and local craftwork.

11:00am Continue the journey to **③** Anse Royale, the lively and main 'town' in south Mahé. Explore the small **fish market** on the roadside. If you like you can enjoy a refreshing dip in the sea away from the fishing boats. From November to May the beach is perfect for swimming and snorkelling. Food and drinks are available from the beach restaurant **Kaz Kreol** *(daily | tel. 437 16 80 | Budget)*. The location is fantastic, although unfortunately service and quality are rather mixed. Opposite in the small shop in **INSIDERTIP** **Coco Creole** you should definitely look at the attractive souvenirs!

Enchanted rainforest vegetation in the hinterlands of Anse Intendance

02:00pm Now continue about **8 km/5 mi south along the increasingly deserted coast road. Shortly before you reach the southern tip, the road curves sharply to the right and heads across the mountains towards Quatre Bornes,** a mountain village, which has kept its unspoiled charm. **At the village entrance, take a sharp left turn off the mini-roundabout. Follow this steeply winding road downhill. At the first major road crossing, turn right onto Intendance Road. Drive straight on past the entrance to the Hotel Banjan Tree on the right. Now, continue on an untarmacked road with plenty of potholes to ④ Anse Intendance → p. 37. Behind a small car park a tiny track leads to the bay,** which ranks internationally as one of the world's most beautiful bays. Swimming is prohibited here due to dangerous undercurrents, but a stroll along the sandy beach is unforgettable! Finally, enjoy a coffee on the terrace of

8 km/5 mi

④ Anse Intendance

2

St. Louis ⚓ **Victoria** ①

○ *Île Moyenne*

Île Longue

Île au Cerf

Pier Ward

Botanical Garden

Trois Frères 699

⚓ Eden Island

Morne Seychellois 905

Morne Seychellois N.P.

497

Providence

Morne Blanc 675

La Misère

Exotic Garden Centre

Île Anonyme

Port Glaud

★ *Exotic Garden Centre*

✈

Grand Anse

Mt. Harrison 580

Pointe la Rue

Grand Anse

Capucins

Île aux Vaches

Anse Boileau

Mte. Brulée 501

②

Boileau Bay

Pointe au Sel

Anse à la Mouche

⑦

③

Anse Royale

⑥

⑤

Spice Garden

Baie Lazare

Mont Parnel 378

Quatre Bornes

④

2 km
1.24 mi

10.5 km/6.5 mi

the Hotel **Banjan Tree** at the northern end of the beach – a breathtaking panorama is guaranteed!

From Anse Intendance head back on the same road up to Quatre Bornes and turn left here in a north-easterly direction and descend to the coast road, first heading via Takamaka and Baie Lazare to Anse aux Poules Bleues. Just before the beach, stop at the ⑤ **studio of Michael Adams**, the most famous Seychellois artist. Look at his colourful and fantastical paintings in the exhibition area on his property, which is filled with plenty of animals. **From here, drive a few metres along the coast road heading north and then turn left into the**

⑤ Studio of Michael Adams 🏛 🛍

0.5 km/0.3 mi

next small street. **Behind a dark palm forest on the right you will find the** 🌀 ⑥ **Pineapple Studio** *(Mon–Sat 10am–18pm | Anse aux Poules Bleues)*. Here you can find hand-made soaps, towels, printed T-shirts and the finest artisan jewellery.

`05:00pm` To finish off the tour **drive back along the coast road and follow it further northwards** where at ⑦ **Anse à la Mouche** you can take a long stroll along the white sandy beach and paddle in the crystal clear, calm water. Pure indulgence! Later in the afternoon when the sun is setting you can enjoy a chilled drink on the other side of the road at the **Anchor Café** *(closed Sun | tel. 437 12 89 | Budget)*. You should try the 'blacked fish' with exotic spices. **Then, head north to the next junction and head to the right into the heart of the countryside on Les Canelles Road.**

On the winding mountain road make your descent back to Anse Royale on the east coast. Turn left here onto the coast road which takes you back again to ① **Victoria.**

⑥ Pineapple Studio 🛍

1 km/0.6 mi

⑦ Anse à la Mouche 🚶 🏖 🍴 🍹

24 km/14.9 mi

① Victoria

The sand and sea cannot be whiter and clearer than here at Anse à la Mouche

3

ASCENT TO NID D'AIGLE ON LA DIGUE

START: ❶ Calou Guesthouse END: ❶ Calou Guesthouse	½ day Actual walking time approx. 2½ hours
Distance: 🚶 approx. 5 km/3.1 mi	

COSTS: Overnight stay in ❶ **Calou Guesthouse** approx. 2,000 rupees for double room, snacks and drinks in the Bellevue approx. 230 rupees/person

WHAT TO PACK: sturdy, but not too heavy walking shoes, drinking water, sun screen

IMPORTANT TIPS: Due to the strong sunshine, mornings are better for hiking. Please do not attempt the tour straight after a tropical rainstorm. Opening hours of the snack restaurant ❷ **Bellevue** depend on the weather. Please enquire with the locals before setting off, or call the tour operator: *tel. 252 78 56*. A good guide for hikes on La Digue is Robert Agnes from *Sunny Trail Guides (Tel. 252 53 57 | www.sunnytrailguide.net)*.

A beautiful and gentle hike takes you to La Digue and the Nid d'Aigle, the 'eagle's nest', where you will be rewarded with a breathtaking panoramic view after the tiring ascent.

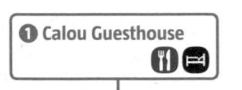

❶ Calou Guesthouse

To be ready to set off early in the morning, stopover the night before at ❶ **Calou Guesthouse** → p. 58. This small guesthouse is a snug, family-oriented establishment. Delicious creole food is also served here – detailed explanations are given of the dishes that are served at a long table.

09:00am Next morning, after an early breakfast set off on foot **along the 'main street' – the Calou Guesthouse is on the left – in a southerly direction to the centre of the island. After just 5 minutes you will see the Hotel Chateau St Cloud on the left. The route to the summit of the Nid d'Aigle begins 5 minutes later at a fork in the road at the central part of the island** which is known as La Réunion. **From here, a small road on the left heads eastwards into the mountainous centre of the island. Although there are numerous trails through the tropical vegetation to the summit – please follow the small route!** Even the locals don't exactly know the path through the forest. Now the real climb starts up to the mountain; the 2.5 km/1.6 mile-long ascent is steep. The high humidity and heat, which you already feel early on, can make the ascent seem exhausting. It's best to take things gently and admire the tropical flowers and plants on the side of the path. The tarmac route winds up the mountain face; **keep left at the first bend and right at the second.** There is hardly any shade, but take a short break at the end of the tarmac road: the small, rather improvised snack restaurant ❷ **Bellevue** not only promises a fabulous view but also offers freshly squeezed exotic juices and fabulous fruit cocktails – perfect energy drinks for the last part of the climb. To make the ascent to the summit, which begins after Bellevue,

2 km/1.2 mi

❷ Bellevue

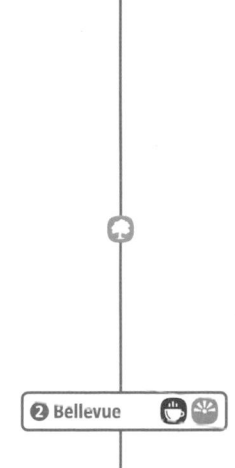

Popular photo motif: La Digue's smooth granite cliffs

0.5 km/0.3 mi

leave the tarmac path and use a small trail. This may be in a better or worse condition, depending on the weather. After prolonged rain showers, the eroded red earth often becomes a slippery channel.

❸ Nid d'Aigle 🗺️

11:00am After about half an hour (depending on the heat and condition) the summit is in sight: **❸ Nid d'Aigle**, the 'eagle's nest'. At an altitude of 333 m/1,093 ft, you are standing in the middle of the blue of sky and sea! Enjoy the sensational view across La Digue and the unique panoramic view of Praslin! The other offshore small islands also make fabulous photo opportunities. When you've had enough of admiring everything and recovered a little, **make the descent on the same route back to the ❶ Calou Guesthouse**.

2.5 km/1.6 mi

❶ Calou Guesthouse

4 MOUNTAINS AND TROPICAL FOREST ON MAHÉ

START: ❶ Victoria	1 day
END: ❶ Victoria	Driving time 1½, actual walking time (2 km/1.2 mi) 1½ hours
Distance: 🚗 35 km/21.8 mi	

COSTS: approx. 770 rupees for car hire, approx. 150 rupees for petrol, approx. 460 rupees/person for meals, if necessary approx. 1,100 rupees for the mountain guide
WHAT TO PACK: hiking shoes, swim wear, sun screen

IMPORTANT TIPS: swim wear, sturdy walking shows for the hike, if required, walking sticks, plenty of drinking water, insect repellent for the forest, sun screen for the summit
For less experienced hikers, it is recommended to book a mountain guide for the ascent to ❹ Copolia, e.g. *Belle's Tour Guiding (tel. 272 24 92 | terence.belle@yahoo.com)*
❻ Tea Factory: Closed Sat/Sun, it is best to arrange the guided tour in advance: *tel. 437 82 21*

Immerse yourself in the tropical mountain region of the Seychelles with a hike through the cloud forest, discover rare plants and animals and follow the trails of former settlers.

❶ Victoria

08:00am Leave ❶ Victoria → p. 41 just before the botanical gardens heading west on Liberation Avenue, and after the first turn follow the road through the suburb of Bel Air heading left in a southerly direction on **Sans Souci Road**, later leading to **Fôret Noire Road. After about 15 minutes on the steep mountain road** on the right you reach the gleaming white wellness hotel ❷ **Copolia Lodge** *(Fôret Noire Road | tel. 422 53 72 | www.copolialodge.com)*, where you should definitely try (and buy) some of the fantastic local INSIDER TIP organic cosmetic products by YiKing.

Park your hire care parallel to the hotel or street and on the left follow the green-yellow sign to the adventurous ❸ **Copolia Trail**, a hiking trail, which first makes a steep descent and passes a stream before making an ascent (very steep in parts) over eroded cliffs and roots. **The shady path is usually easy to make out: if in doubt, keep to the (few) yellow, horizontal route markers.** Breathe in the fragrance of cinnamon and clove in the enchanted forest. If you're lucky and keep a close watch you will see the world's smallest frogs and stick insects! After 2 km/1.2 mi

5.5 km / 3.4 mi

❷ Copolia Lodge

0.3 km / 0.2 mi

❸ Copolia Trail

0.7 km / 0.4 mi

Meat-eating plants grow on the plateau of Mount Copolia

❹ Copolia

3 km/1.9 mi

❺ Mission Lodge

2.5 km/1.6 mi

❻ Tea Factory

(approx. 1.5 hours) you will reach a small cliff face that you climb with the help of a ladder. Now you have arrived on a vast granite plateau, the summit of **❹ Copolia** almost at an altitude of 500 m/1,640 ft. Marvel at the hedge here with the tropical meat-eating pitcher plants, and enjoy the fantastic view of the capital city, its harbour and off-shore islands. Be careful: don't walk to close the edge of the cliff – falling hazard! **Continue on the same trail back to the car at Copolia Lodge.**

12:00pm Then, you follow – past the residence of the Seychellois president (the small round tower on the left) – the longest mountain road on Mahé for approx. 10 minutes to **❺ Mission Lodge**. From the car park it's just a few steps to the ruins of a former missionary station dating from the emancipation of the slaves (18th century). From the **viewing platform** you enjoy a breathtaking view over the Morne Seychellois National Park and the western coast with its offshore islands. **Follow the picturesque mountain road westwards** and cross the tropical timber forest and numerous tea plantations. **After only 10 mins. on the left** is the **❻ Tea Factory**. Arrange a guided tour to view the plantation; at the end of the tour you can taste a cup of tea.

01:30pm The mountain road heads westwards to the coast. Turn right towards Port Glaud and after less than

Tea factory: picking tea leaves is tiring work by hand

a kilometre you can enjoy a late lunch by the sea at the restaurant **❼ Del Place** *(daily 11am–23pm | Port Glaud | tel. 2814111 | Moderate)*. On the wooden deck you float above the water and can enjoy tasty fish dishes or light snacks. Why not go for a swim? You have your swim wear – some steps lead straight into the refreshing, shallow water!

04:00pm **Drive back to Port Glaud and head south here on the coast road until after 5 km/3.1 mi you reach the** impressive bay of **❽ Grand' Anse**. Here, you can park at the school sports ground and enjoy a short stroll along the beach. Unfortunately, swimming is strictly prohibited due to the dangerous currents. **From here, continue southwards to the next big crossroads and at the petrol station take the left turnoff towards the mountains. An impressive mountain road with forests on either side brings you back via La Misère to ❶ Victoria.**

---

5 km/3.1 mi

❼ Del Place 🍴 🏊

5 km/3.1 mi

❽ Grand' Anse 🚶 🌳

10.5 km/6.5 mi

🌳

❶ Victoria

SPORTS & ACTIVITIES

There is far more to the Seychelles than the water sports so often associated with this travel destination.
Nonetheless, the recreational activities available are limited to a reasonable level in order not to put any unnecessary strain on the environment and the guests that are seeking peace and quiet. The larger hotels offer sports and fitness facilities such as tennis and squash.

ANGLING & FISHING

The rich fishing grounds of the Seychelles are very attractive to fishermen. On the beaches of the main islands there are numerous well established boat rental companies that offer half or full day fishing trips. The costs lie between 4,600 rupees (half day) and 15,400 rupees (full day), depending on the type of boat and the equipment. The waters off Bird and Denis Islands are fabulous for fishing as this is where the seabed drops off more than 1,800 m/5,900 ft. The Alphonse, Desroches and North Islands are popular with fly fishermen *(info: www.seyfly. sc)*. For coastal fishing the best areas are the lagoons and cliffs on the south coast of Mahé and no fishing permits are necessary. In April and October fishing competitions are held on the Seychelles.

CYCLING

Whilst bicycles on Mahé are not an ideal mode of transport (the streets are con-

The crystal clear water and beautiful marine world of the Indian Ocean make the islands a popular choice for divers and snorkellers

gested and there are no designated cycling trails) on La Digue and Praslin the bicycle is part of daily life for locals as well as tourists. Rentals are available on La Digue at the harbour and on Praslin at Côte d'Or and Grand' Anse.

GOLF

The Seychelles only became an attractive travel destination for golfers after the opening of an ● 🏌 18 hole course in the north of Praslin (Anse Kerlan), prior to that the small 9 hole course at the *Reef Hotel (Anse aux Pins | tel. 437 62 52)* on Mahé was the only option available. The 18 hole course has some spectacular views of the world's most beautiful beaches. For the mandatory greenfee, the course is also open to non-guests of the hotel through the *Lémuria Resort (tel. 428 12 81)*. It's not essential to bring your own golf clubs which can be hired at the resort. Some hotels also offer lessons with golf pros.

HIKING

When the weather is not good for swimming you can take some time to get to know the islands from another perspective, by going on some hikes through the scenic and varied country-

HORSEBACK RIDING

A 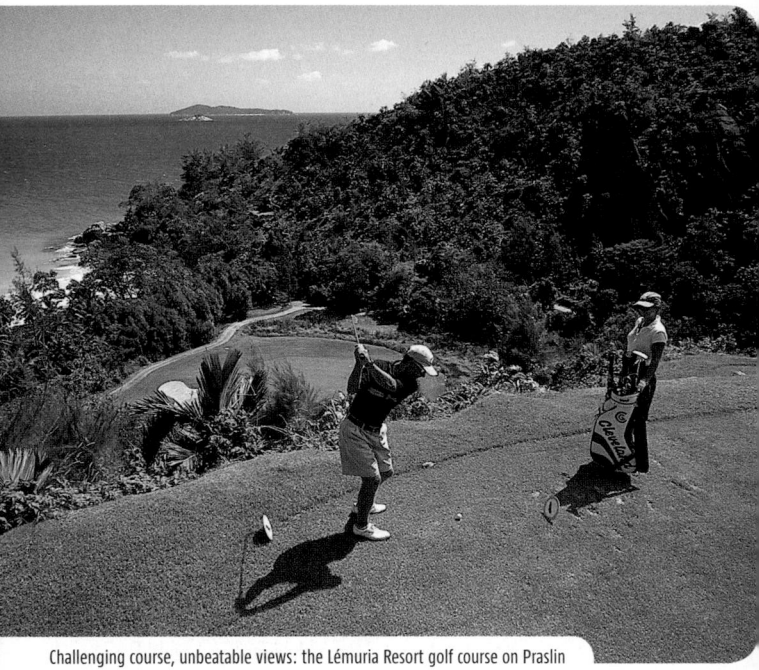 **INSIDER TIP** beach ride on an Arabian horse is also possible for less experienced riders. On the main island of Mahé you can try the *Utegangar Riding Centre (at the Le Meridien Barbarons Hotel | dai-*

Challenging course, unbeatable views: the Lémuria Resort golf course on Praslin

side. There are a few hikes detailed in the section on Mahé but you can do a hike on just about every island as there are no dangerous animals to worry about. You will need some sturdy walking shoes and bear in mind that even the designated trails may be partially overgrown. However, the authorities have promised that the most important trails on Mahé will be well-maintained in the future.

ly 8am–6pm | tel. 471 23 55 | utegangar@ gmail.com). On La Digue you can go riding at *L'Union Estate (daily 8am–3pm | tel. 423 42 40)* near Cliff Ladouceur. For both riding centres it is recommended that you first make a telephonic reservation.

SCUBA DIVING & SNORKELLING

The Seychelles is one of the most beautiful diving sites on earth. The best times are the months at the turn of the monsoon, April/May and Oct/Nov, when the sea is calm and clear. There are diving centres at almost all the larger hotels. An individual dive starts from 600 rupees (without equipment) but they also offer dives with equipment as well as nitrox diving. A PADI diving course costs 5,400–6,100 rupees. A rather unique attraction is a INSIDER TIP dive with some large (but harmless) whale sharks, they can be found in the waters between October and April. *Seychelles Underwater Centre | P. O. Box 384 | tel. 434 54 45 | www. diveseychelles.com.sc*

The following waters are ideal for snorkelling: the Ste Anne and Port Launay National Parks off Mahé, off Côte d'Or and Anse Lazio on Praslin, as well as the area off the smaller island around Praslin (such as St Pierre) and off the west coast of La Digue. If you haven't brought your own equipment, you can rent it on site for a lending fee.

SURFING

The Seychelles is only suitable for surfing under certain conditions. Some good surfing spots on Mahé in the middle of the year are *Anse aux Poules Bleues* and *Carana Beach* while *Grand' Anse* and *Soleil d'Or* are good at the end of the year; also, depending on weather conditions, *Anse Kerlan* on Praslin and *Grand' Anse* on La Digue.

SWIMMING

However beautiful they look, not all of the waters off the Seychelles are suitable for swimming. The beaches with dangerous and unpredictable currents always have multilingual signs warning of the dangers. A far less dangerous obstacle whilst swimming is that some beaches are so shallow during some seasons that the water barely covers your feet. Good swimming beaches on Mahé are the popular *Beau Vallon Bay*, *Anse à la Mouche* (with its protective coral reef) and the scenic *Anse Intendance* (strong breakers sometimes). On Praslin there is the endless *Anse Volbert* which is best from May to September. The granite boulders that frame *Anse la Source à Jean* offer a beautiful background for swimming and sun bathing. Equally attractive are the beaches on the east coast of La Digue *(Grand' Anse, Petite Anse, Anse Cocos)*, which are however, not protected by reefs. Anse Cocos is often considered one of the world's most beautiful beaches.

WATER SPORTS

The water sports centres are along the bay of *Beau Vallon* on Mahé and the *Côte d'Or* on Praslin. Most of the accommodation on the Outer Islands also have their own water sports centres. Facilities include jet-skiing, kayaking, waterskiing and parasailing.

WELLNESS

Recuperation for body and mind – spa offers are now available in almost all larger hotels. This not only includes fairly extensive offers of classic massages but also yoga, Tai-chi or Hatha yoga courses with professional instructors. If you take your well-being seriously, you can combine your Seychelles holiday with an Indian Ayurveda spa. The hotels also have fitness centres with equipment like treadmills and plenty of power-training machines.

TRAVEL WITH KIDS

The Seychelles are not only ideal for a holiday but also a paradise for children – not least because it is one of the few countries in the tropics that doesn't require additional vaccinations and where there are practically no dangerous animals and plants.

The Seychelles are a family-friendly holiday destination and if you are travelling with your offspring the locals may approach for a friendly chat, with the older ones often patting the children on their heads. You won't find people frowning at you if your child behaves the way children behave, by playing loudly or kicking up a fuss.

ACCOMMODATION

When choosing your accommodation, it is worth noting that some hotels have locations that are not suitable for children – such as the *Sunset Beach Hotel* on Mahé, which is on a rocky outcrop right on the sea. These hotels usually have a prescribed minimum age. On the other hand, some large hotels offer special entertainment programmes for their younger guests as well as a babysitter service for those parents who need some time alone.

Some hotels also offer family suites, most have cots available and many hotels have space for an extra bed for an older child. If children want their own rooms, larger hotels have adjacent rooms with connecting doors. Travel agencies usually indicate these options in their catalogues.

The high-end category of hotels also have offers especially geared to the needs of children such as the *Lémuria Resort,* which has a playground and offers different options for older children and teenagers.

ATTRACTIONS

On Mahé it is worth taking the children on a visit to the *Botanical Gardens* (see p. 42) and older children will enjoy exploring the *Jardin du Roi* (see p. 37) where you can explain to them where spices come from, which most only know in their processed form in their kitchen cupboards. The same goes for the *Tea Factory* (see p. 48) on Mahé, where they can experience the growing, harvesting and processing of tea, while the *L'Union Estate* (see p. 57) on La Digue demonstrates the processing of coconuts. If you are staying on

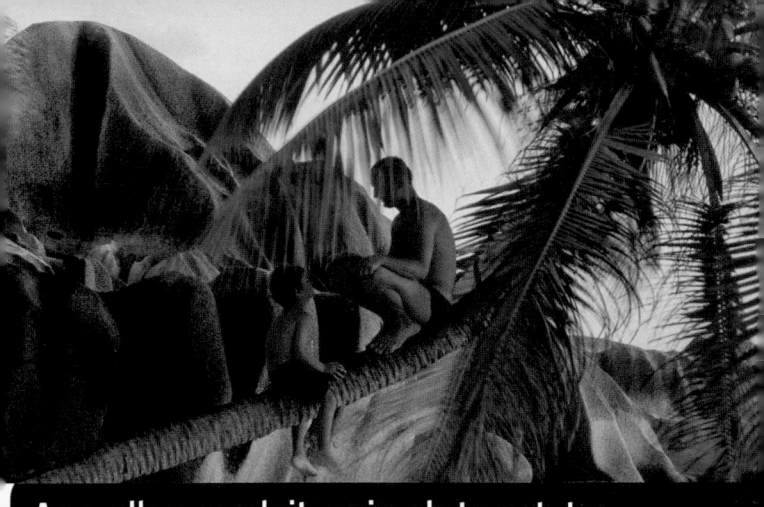

An endless sandpit, animals to pet, tea and coconut harvests – the Seychelles is more nature park than an amusement park

Praslin, you should book a day trip by boat to the neighbouring islands of Cousin and Curieuse, where you are guaranteed to **INSIDER TIP** encounter giant tortoises and all kinds of exotic birds and the tortoises don't mind if you pet them.

BEACHES

The one danger to children is the harsh, equatorial sun and even the lush vegetation offers little in the way of protection from its rays. If you have taken the necessary precautions (a hat and a tee shirt even while swimming!) then the endless, sandy beaches are an absolute pleasure. The bright sand is fine, powdery and usually very clean.

In many places the beaches have very shallow waters that are ideal for children but you should always be on the lookout for the waves and take the sign-posted warnings very seriously. It is also a good idea to have beach sandals with

non-slip soles as some of the beaches have sharp-edged corals that can cause nasty injuries.

DIVING

Even though a minimum age of 12 years is mandatory for participation in the dive courses, the underwater world need not be denied to younger children. From 8 years of age they can participate in a *Bubblemaker* course where they learn how to use a mask and snorkel. Those 12 years and older can do the *Junior PADI Open Water Diver Certificate*. It is important to remember that your children need to obtain a diving medical certificate from a sports physician prior to departure. Glass bottom boat trips are available on Mahé and other islands. Without getting your feet wet, you can observe corals, fish and other marine creatures up close.

FESTIVALS & EVENTS

There are a thousand reasons to celebrate: this is the motto that the residents of the Seychelles live by and their positive attitude towards life is very contagious. One such expression of their zest for life is the Sega, a dance whose origin is found in nearby Africa. The genuine Sega can however only be seen on the more remote islands. A modern version with the latest disco rhythms is danced in the clubs on Mahé. Then there are the Kamtole dances, which have a lot in common with the American Square Dance and the Scottish Reel, but actually come from France, where they were called Contredanse. The dance has a so-called commander who calls out which steps are danced. Another popular dance is the Moutia, which was originally the songs of slaves. The dance received a bad reputation, because – particularly in the eyes of the clergy – the movements were sometimes suggestive and lewd. The Moutia is usually spontaneously danced at night under an open sky. The goatskin drums are first warmed and stretched at a fire and the firelight makes the dancers and their movements seem shrouded in a ghostly light.

FESTIVALS

You can rely on the fact that there will always be INSIDER TIP *spontaneous street festivals* somewhere on one of the islands, in one of the villages.

Even ● *going to church on Sunday* becomes a festival, perhaps because there isn't much variety during the week. The well dressed churchgoers all file out to church. Since almost all inhabitants of the Seychelles are Catholic, the various church festivals also play a particularly important role.

There are solemn ★ ● *processions* on Assumption Day; the inhabitants of La Digue are particularly famous for their picturesque processions.

The *anniversary of the coup d'état* on 5 June and the *Independence Day* on 29 June – are both celebrated with parades in Victoria on Mahé and with various other festivities (sport competitions, children's festivals etc).

EVENTS

The most significant festival on the Seychelles is the ★ *Carnival International*, which attracts thousands of visitors to Victoria on the first weekend

Pure joie de vivre: the Seychellois are a happy folk – even the Sunday church service is a very festive occasion

in March. The highlight is the procession with a float that commemorates the first settlement on the Seychelles. Carnival groups are invited from all over the world.

In October the week long ★ *Festival Kreol* takes place on Mahé with traditional dances and Creole music. The festival combines folklore with academic research (mainly by the *Lenstiti Kreol* institute on Anse aux Pins). Further highlights are the music show *Lakadans*, fashion shows *(Defile Lanmod)* and the Sunday at the sea *(Dimans Kreol Bor Lanmer)* on Beau Vallon beach on Mahé.

In honour of the Hindu elephant god *Vinayagar* a festival takes place in September in the Arulmikunavasakkthi Temple in Victoria. And in October there is also a *Deepavali Festival* in honour of the Hindu goddess Lakshmi.

The INSIDER TIP *SUBIOS Underwater Festival* (Oct/Nov) combines diving and snorkelling during the day with slide shows, film and video presentations and other events in various hotels in the evening. Information: *www.subios.com*

PUBLIC HOLIDAYS

1/2 January	New Year
March/April	Good Friday
1 May	Labour Day
May/June	Corpus Christi
5 June	Liberation Day
18 June	Constitution Day
29 June	National Day
15 August	Assumption of Mary/ La Digue Festival
1 November	All Saints' Day
8 December	Immaculate Conception of Virgin Mary
25 December	Christmas Day

If a public holiday is on a Sunday, the next Monday is holiday in lieu

LINKS, BLOGS, APPS & MORE

www.seychelles.travel/en The official website of the Seychelles Tourist Board. Very informative site, nicely done and well maintained. Lots of information about the island's nature, climate, itinerary ideas, events and an interactive gallery and videos

www.natureseychelles.org An excellent site for those interested in the conservation activities on the Seychelles

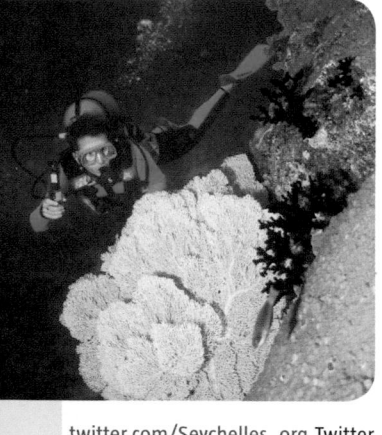

www.lonelyplanet.com/thorntree Forum to exchange travel information and ask advice. After your trip, you can post your own evaluations, photos and reports

www.tripwolf.com/en Travel tips, activities, photos, blogs and evaluations from the travel community. Background reports and the possibility of direct bookings of accommodation

www.seychellesweekly.com Weekly online newspaper with, sports and cultural events, news, politics and the weather

twitter.com/Seychelles_org Twitter account by So Seychelles with regular information about nature conservation, travel news and images and also retweets from the tourism board

www.youtube.com/watch?v=OIcNpUW1oxA A taste of paradise, this video touches on the geography, history and culture of the Seychelles

www.youtube.com/watch?v=4AHkKYUKiHQ&feature=related Video impressions of the colourful culture of the Seychelles, with a section about the annual *Creole Festival* celebration that takes place in October

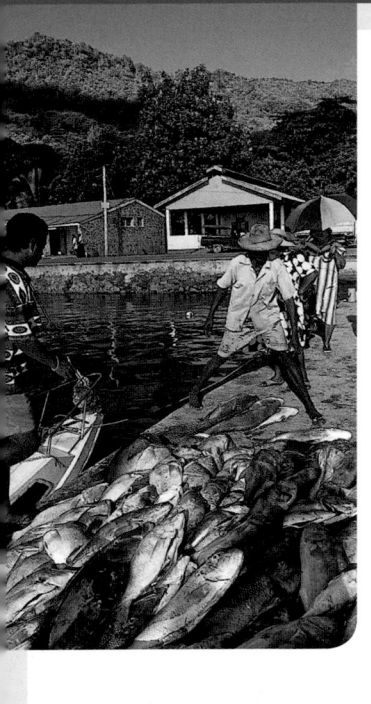

www.youtube.com/watch?v=YhtBt7CCc3U&feature=related A video by the *Seychelles Tourist Board* with fantastic shots of the beaches, dive sites, wildlife, landscape and other sightseeing attractions on the Seychelles

www.youtube.com/watch?v=HdibaJMnuVs Beautifully shot video showcasing Mahé, Praslin and La Digue's beaches

www.youtube.com/watch?v=BgtDDspdXVc Great video about all the excellent dive opportunities offered by the underwater world of the Seychelles, with detailed dive information

short.travel/sey10 Music video site with Sega dance routines for the song "Bake Yaya" by the Seychellois popular singer Jean Marc Volcy

short.travel/sey11 Film with background music advertising the Seychelles with beautiful countryside, animal and underwater photos (30 mins.)

APPS

Seychelles Islands Free App guide to the Seychelles with many current events, useful info, news, weather forecasts and GPS-supported maps

Seychelles Islands Travel Guide – Mobile Travel App with photos, info, maps (GPS), search function that serves as a complete travel planning tool

Seychelles GPS Map Navigator App by Flytomap is an offline navigation app with maps (GPS) and satellite pictures to navigate throughout the country and plan your trip

Seychelles E-Travel This App from the *Seychelles Tourism Board* features six headings: short island descriptions, maps of the main islands, activities, events, travel information, contact details of the Seychelles tour offices

TRAVEL TIPS

ARRIVAL

The Seychelles are serviced by national lines such as *Air Seychelles (www.airsey chelles.com)* and *British Airways (www. britishairways.com)* as well as via European hubs such as Amsterdam or Paris. The flight from London to Mahé takes about 10 hours. There are also flights via the Gulf with airlines such as *Qatar Airways (www.qatarairways.com)* or *Emirates (www.emirates.com/uk)* via Dubai. The Seychelles International Airport on Mahé lies in the centre of the island on the east coast. Almost every place on Mahé is within an hour's taxi ride from here. When flying onward to other islands you need to take into account the luggage weight restrictions (10–15 kg/22–33 lbs) as you will be charged if your luggage is overweight. Air Seychelles has connecting flights to Alphonse, Bird, Denis, Desroches, Frégate and North Islands, but these flights are treated as charter flights and need to be booked by the your travel operator.

BANKS & CURRENCY EXCHANGE

The import and export of local currency is limited to 2,000 rupees (approx. £ 115/US$ 148). There are banks in the capital Victoria (Mon–Fri usually 8am–2pm, Sat 8am–11am) and there are airport exchange counters. You can also change money at your hotel reception, however, the rate will be worse. There are ATMs on Mahé at the airport, in Victoria and at Anse Royale as well as on Praslin and La Digue. The exchange of Seychellios rupees is only done on presentation of your original exchange receipt. You will need local cash for small purchases and if you want to take a taxi. All major credit cards are widely accepted and can be used to pay for hotels and restaurants, to hire car services and for making cash withdrawals.

RESPONSIBLE TRAVEL

It doesn't take a lot to be environmentally friendly whilst travelling. Don't just think about your carbon footprint whilst flying to and from your holiday destination but also about how you can protect nature and culture abroad. As a tourist it is especially important to respect nature, look out for local products, cycle instead of driving, save water and much more. If you would like to find out more about eco-tourism please visit: *www.ecotourism.org*

CAR HIRE

You can rent a car on Mahé and Praslin (minimum age 21 years) on presentation of your national driver's licence (drive on the left). The vehicle can be delivered to your hotel, but there are also plenty of rental companies at the airport. There are numerous car rental companies and it is worth comparing prices. Remember to document any previous damages to the car when you take over the vehicle. You can expect to pay about 845 rupees per day excluding petrol.

The road network on Mahé and Praslin is well developed, but the roads often lack a guard rail, something that can be quite dangerous as the side of the road often falls off sharply and if you swerve you can land in the ditch off the road. Maximum speed in town 40 km/h/25 mph, out of town 65 km/h/40 mph.

CONSULATES & EMBASSIES

BRITISH HIGH COMMISSION
3rd Floor, Oliaji Trade Centre | Francis Rachel Street | Victoria | Mahé | Tel. +248 428 36 66 | bhcvictoria@fco.gov.uk

CONSULAR AGENCY OF THE UNITED STATES OF AMERICA
2nd Floor, Oliaji Trade Centre | Francis Rachel Street | Victoria | Mahé | Tel. +248 422 52 56 | usconsular@seychelles.net

CUSTOMS

Your duty free allowance includes the import of 200 cigarettes, 2 L of spirits and 2 L wine as well as items intended for your personal consumption. Weapons (including spear guns) and ammunition are strictly prohibited as well as all kinds of seeds, plants, animal products, tea and the likes. Drugs and all forms of pornography are forbidden.

You may not export tortoise shells and corals and written permission is required to export coco de mer (available from authorised sellers). The following goods can be exported duty-free when you leave the Seychelles: 200 cigarettes or 50 cigars or 250 g tobacco, 1 L of spirits or 4 L wine, 250 g coffee and other goods up to a value of £ 340/430 euros. Travellers to the US who are residents of the country do not have to pay duty on articles purchased overseas up to the value of US$ 800, but there are limits on the amount of alcoholic beverages and tobacco products. For the regulations for international travel for US residents please see *www.cbp.gov.*

Returning travellers from the UK can bring in goods worth up to £ 390. For the limits on alcoholic beverages and tobacco products please see www.gov.uk/duty-free-goods.

ELECTRICITY

The voltage is 240 volt AC 50 Hz. The standard plugs are British three pin so

CURRENCY CONVERTER

£	SCR	SCR	£
1	17.75	10	0.55
3	53.25	30	1.65
5	88.75	50	2.75
13	230.75	130	7.15
40	710	400	22
75	1,331.25	750	41.25
120	2,130	1,200	66
250	4,437.50	2,500	137.50
500	8,875	5,000	275

$	SCR	SCR	$
1	13.55	10	0.75
3	40.65	30	2.25
5	67.75	50	3.75
13	176.15	130	9.75
40	542	400	30
75	1,016.25	750	56.25
120	1,626	1,200	90
250	3,387.50	2,500	187.50
500	6,775	5,000	375
500	6,775	5,000	375

For current exchange rates see www.xe.com

visitors from other countries will need an adaptor and voltage converter which you can get at the hotel reception or in shops in Victoria.

EMERGENCY SERVICES

Police, fire brigade, doctor and ambulance: *tel. 999*

HEALTH

If you are coming from Europe, vaccinations are not required. However, if you travel via Central Africa, a certificate of immunisation against yellow fever is mandatory. Be careful during the first days of your stay: The sun is intense and can cause severe sunburns even in overcast skies. You should use sun screen with a high sun protection factor. Insect repellent is also useful as on wet days and during the evenings insects can become a nuisance.

On Mahé, La Digue, Praslin and Silhouette there are relatively well equipped hospitals. In the hospital on Mahé *(Mont Fleuri | tel. 437 12 22)* complicated operations are possible, and there is also a 24-hour emergency service. For all islands the emergency number is *999*. Whilst locals are treated in hospital for free, foreign visitors have to pay for treatment so travel insurance is advisable, which includes a return flight should it be required. There are pharmacies on all inhabited islands.

Since 2015, silkmoths have invaded Mahé (the locals call them senir plim). The hairlets of this moth that are dis persed on the wind the insects nest mainly in mango trees and terrace plants – can lead to a bad skin rash with itchy spots. Pack antihistamines and hydrocortisone cream. In worst cases, fever, shivering and breathlessness can result.

Every large bay has a clinic that can also help with cortisone injections.

IMMIGRATION

At arrivals you need a passport which is valid at least until the day of the scheduled departure, a valid return or onward ticket and sufficient funds for accommodation: approx. 2,300 rupees/day, in cash or as travellers' cheques or credit cards; random checks are carried out. Package tourists do not require such documentation. On arrival you are given a visitor's permit, which is valid for 30 month and can be extended during this time at the *Department of Immigration (Independence House | Mahé | tel. +24 84 29 36 36 | info@immigration. gov.sc)* for up to twelve months. Children require their own passport with photograph. There is no longer a passenger service charge, it is now included in the fare.

INFORMATION

SEYCHELLES TOURIST OFFICE UK
130–132 Buckhingham Palace Road, ground floor | London | SW1W 9SA | tel. +44 (0) 20 72 45 61 06 | seychelles@uk sto.co.uk | www.seychel les.travel | Mon– Fri 9am–5pm
LOCAL SEYCHELLES TOURIST OFFICE
– Mahé | Headquarters STB | Espace Building | P. O. Box 1262 | Victoria | Mahé | tel. 467 13 00 | info@seychelles.travel | Mon–Fri 8am–4pm, Sat/Sun closed
– Mahé | Independence House | Victoria | Mahé | tel. 461 08 00 | info@seychelles. net | Mon–Fri 8am–4.30pm, Sat 9am– noon, closed Sundays
– Mahé | Seychelles International Airport | Point Larue | Mahé | tel. 437 31 36 | stbair port@seychelles.net | for arriving international flights

– La Passe | La Digue | tel. 423 43 93 | stbladigue@seychelles.travel | Mon–Fri 8am–5pm, Sat 9am–noon, public holidays 9am–noon, closed Sundays
– Baie Ste Anne | Praslin | Jetty, Bai Ste Anne | tel. 423 26 69 | stbpraslin@seychelles.net | Mon–Fri 8am–4pm, Sat 8am–noon, public holidays 8am–noon, closed Sundays

INTERNET CAFÉS & WI-FI

On the Seychelles there are three Internet service providers, which each have an Internet café in Victoria (approx. 31 rupees 15 min):
– Doubleclick Seychelles | Maison la Rosière | Victoria | tel. 422 47 96 | doubleclicksey@gmail.com
– Incipe Seychelles | 6&7 MS Complex | Revolution Avenue | Victoria | tel. 426 66 99 | office@incipe.com
– Kokonet Café | Pirates Arms Building | Independence Avenue | Victoria | tel. 447 47 47 | kokonet@seychelles.sc
There are other Internet cafés on Praslin and La Digue. The more expensive hotels offer their guests either PCs with Internet connection or Wi-Fi hotspots with connection in your room or areas like the hotel reception, lobby or bar. However, the speed is slow and broadband is not yet available in the Seychelles.

NUDISM

There are no designated nudist beaches. However, topless bathing is generally tolerated.

PERSONAL SAFETY

The Seychelles are a safe tourist destination. However, like everywhere else you should take the usual security precautions – avoid displaying valuable items

and e.g. stay away from the drug scene on the beaches.

PHONE & MOBILE PHONE

You can make direct calls from hotels and from the public pay phones. Calls from hotels are expensive, it is cheaper from public telephones. Phone cards are available at the main post office, in many shops on Mahé or at telephone companies such as *Airtel* and *Cable &*

BUDGETING

Lemonade	£0.35/$0.45 for a shop bought bottle
Coco de mer	£130–260/$175–350 for a legally exportable coco de mer
Wine	£20/$30 for a bottle in a restaurant
Hire car	from £45/$60 a day
Pizza	£5/$6.50 at the Pirates Arms Restaurant in Victoria
Day trip	from £90/$115 to a neighbouring island incl. transfer and a meal

Wireless Ltd. For pay phones with coins you need 1 and 5 rupee coins. Dialling codes: *Seychelles: +248 | UK: +44 | USA: +1.* In the Seychelles, there are no codes for the individual islands or towns.
Mobile roaming charges are very expensive. It is cheaper to get a prepaid card; starter packs cost approx. 600 rupees including a credit balance.

POST

The main post office is in Victoria on Independence Avenue, opposite the Clock Tower *(Mon–Fri 8am–4pm, Sat 8am–noon)*. On Praslin there are post offices in Baie Ste Anne and Grande Anse Village *(Mon–Fri 8am–noon, 2pm–4pm, Sat 8am–noon)*. Mailboxes are found in even the smaller towns, but you can also hand in your post at the hotel. Airmail letters and postcards to Europe take around 5 days, a letter (10 g, each additional 10 g 2 rupees) to Europe currently costs 3.50 rupees, a postcard 3 rupees.

PRICES & CURRENCY

The Seychelles currency is the rupee (Seychelles Rupee, SCR). 100 cents is 1 rupee. Bank notes are available in 10, 20, 25, 50, 100 and 500, coins in 1, 5, 10 and 25 cents and 1 and 5 rupees. Restaurant, petrol and taxi fares are on par with those in Europe but bus fares are cheaper. Alcohol, tobacco and luxury goods are expensive. Services (e.g. entrance fees) can be paid in Seychelles rupee (SCR).

PUBLIC TRANSPORT

Buses depart from Victoria for almost all parts of the main island of Mahé (bus station on Palm Street, opposite Unity House). Although there are official timetables, they are only seldom reliable. Particularly at bus stops outside Victoria you should stand on the side of the road and wave to make sure to

WEATHER ON THE SEYCHELLES

	Jan	Feb	March	April	May	June	July	Aug	Sept	Oct	Nov	Dec
Daytime temperatures in °C/°F	28/82	29/84	29/84	30/86	29/84	28/82	27/81	27/81	28/82	28/82	29/84	28/82
Nighttime temperatures in °C/°F	24/75	25/77	25/77	25/77	25/77	25/77	24/75	24/75	24/75	24/75	24/75	24/75
☀	6	6	7	8	8	7	7	7	7	7	7	7
☂	15	10	11	10	9	9	8	7	8	9	12	15
≋	27/81	28/82	28/82	29/84	28/82	27/81	26/79	26/79	26/79	26/79	27/81	27/81

☀ Sunshine hours/day ☂ Precipitation days/month ≋ Water temperature in °C/°F get the driver's attention. There are also buses on Praslin that run daily between 5.30am–10pm, after 6.30pm not as regularly though.

There are *ferries* that commute to Praslin and La Digue several times a day from Inter Island Quay on Mahé. Bookings for the ferry from Praslin to La Digue are via *Inter Island Ferry Service (tel. 423 23 29| www.seychelles.net/iif)*. The high speed catamaran 'Cat Cocos' commutes between Mahé and Praslin *(60 min)* up to three times a day from a terminal on Eden Island, off Mahé over a bridge. Bookings are made via hotel reception or *tel. 432 48 43 or www. catcocos.com*. A real experience is the passage from Mahé to La Digue with the schooner 'La Belle Seraphina' that carries cargo as well as passengers *(tel. 423 23 29)*.

Air Seychelles has *flights* between Mahé and other islands. It is advisable to book well in advance, especially in high season when the flights are often fully booked. Please note that the small aircraft are not suitable for large luggage and there is usually a limit of 10 kg/22 lbs *(Air Seychelles | Victoria | tel. 439 10 00)*.

TAXI

The prices are almost comparable to European countries. The drivers usually speak enough English to understand your destination. No taxis on the Seychelles have taxi meters, so you should ask in advance for the fare price. This is generally too high, but as you have little basis for comparison, it's difficult to negotiate. However, at least this ensures you don't have a nasty surprise... A cheaper alternative is the taxi pirate, i.e. illegal taxis that will take you for half the fare. However, bear in mind

that there is no insurance in the event of an accident!

TIME

The Seychelles is 4 hours ahead of GMT, 3 hours ahead of UK summer time and 2 hours ahead of CET summer time.

TIPPING

Tipping is not obligatory in the Seychelles but rather a sign of appreciation for special services. Of course, waiters, taxi drivers and hotel staff all welcome tips. However, you should not give less than 15 rupees – this could be taken as an insult.

WEATHER, WHEN TO GO

The daytime temperatures are usually between 24 °C/75 °F and 33 °C/91 °F throughout the year. May to October are recommended, and then there is a chance of some overcast days. Most rainfall occurs in December and January, and the driest months are June, July and August.

WHAT TO WEAR

Due to the constant warm temperatures, light summery clothes (such as breathable and easy to wash cottons) can be worn throughout the year. Beach sandals are important as there are sharp corals. Upmarket hotels and restaurants have a dress code and shorts and tee shirts are not an option.

USEFUL PHRASES FRENCH

IN BRIEF

Yes/No/Maybe	oui/non/peut-être
Please/Thank you	s'il vous plaît/merci
Good morning!/afternoon!/ evening!/night!	Bonjour!/Bonjour!/ Bonsoir!/Bonne nuit!
Hello!/goodbye!/See you!	Salut!/Au revoir!/Salut!
Excuse me, please	Pardon!
My name is ...	Je m'appelle ...
I'm from ...	Je suis de ...
May I ...?/ Pardon?	Puis-je ...?/Comment?
I would like to .../ have you got ...?	Je voudrais .../ Avez-vous?
How much is ...?	Combien coûte ...?
I (don't) like this	Ça (ne) me plaît (pas).
good/bad/broken	bon/mauvais/cassé
too much/much/little	trop/beaucoup/peu
all/nothing	tout/rien
Help!/Attention!	Au secours/attention
police/fire brigade/ ambulance	police/pompiers/ ambulance
Could you please help me?	Est-ce que vous pourriez m'aider?
Do you speak English?	Parlez-vous anglais?
Do you understand?	Est-ce que vous comprenez?
Could you please ...?	Pourriez vous ... s'il vous plait?
... repeat that	répéter
... speak more slowly	parler plus lentement
... write that down	l'écrire

DATE & TIME

Monday/Tuesday	lundi/mardi
Wednesday/Thursday	mercredi/jeudi
Friday/Saturday/ Sunday	vendredi/samedi/ dimanche
working day/holiday	jour ouvrable/Jour férié
today/tomorrow/ yesterday	aujourd'hui /demain/ hier
hour/minute	heure/minute
day/night/week	jour/nuit/semaine
month/year	mois/année
What time is it?	Quelle heure est-t-il?

Parlez-vous français?

"Do you speak French?" This guide will help you to say the basic words and phrases in French

It's three o'clock	Il est trois heures
It's half past three.	Il est trois heures et demi
a quarter to four	quatre heures moins le quart

TRAVEL

open/closed	ouvert/fermé
entrance/exit	entrée/sortie
departure/arrival	départ/arrivée
toilets/restrooms /	toilettes/
ladies/gentlemen	femmes/hommes
(no) drinking water	eau (non) potable
Where is ...?/Where are ...?	Où est ...?/Où sont ...?
left/right	à gauche/à droite
straight ahead/back	tout droit/en arrière
close/far	près/loin
bus/tram/underground / taxi/cab	bus/tramway/métro/taxi
stop/cab stand	arrêt/station de taxi
parking lot/parking garage	parking
street map/map	plan de ville/carte routière
train station/harbour/	gare/port/
airport	aéroport
schedule/ticket	horaire/billet
single/return	aller simple/aller-retour
train/track/platform	train/voie/quai
I would like to rent ...	Je voudrais ... louer
a car/a bicycle/	une voiture/un vélo/
a boat	un bateau
petrol/gas station	station d'essence
petrol/gas / diesel	essence/diesel
breakdown/repair shop	panne/garage

FOOD & DRINK

The menu, please	La carte, s'il vous plaît
Could I please have ...?	Puis-je avoir ... s'il vous plaît
bottle/carafe/glass	bouteille/carafe/verre
knife/fork/spoon	couteau/fourchette/cuillère
salt/pepper/sugar	sel/poivre/sucre
vinegar/oil	vinaigre/huile
milk/cream/lemon	lait/crème/citron
cold/too salty/not cooked	froid/trop salé/pas cuit

with/without ice/sparkling	avec/sans glaçons/gaz
vegetarian	végétarien(ne)
May I have the bill, please	Je voudrais payer, s'il vous plaît
bill	addition

SHOPPING

pharmacy/chemist	pharmacie/droguerie
baker/market	boulangerie/marché
shopping centre	centre commercial
department store	grand magasin
100 grammes/1 kilo	cent grammes/un kilo
expensive/cheap/price	cher/bon marché/prix
more/less	plus/moins
organically grown	de l'agriculture biologique

ACCOMMODATION

I have booked a room	J'ai réservé une chambre
Do you have any ... left?	Avez-vous encore ...?
single room/double room	chambre simple/double
breakfast	petit déjeuner
half board/	demi-pension/
full board (American plan)	pension complète
shower/sit-down bath	douche/bain
balcony/terrace	balcon /terrasse
key/room card	clé/carte magnétique
luggage/suitcase/bag	bagages/valise/sac

BANKS, MONEY & CREDIT CARDS

bank/ATM/pin code	banque/guichet automatique/code
cash/credit card	comptant/carte de crédit
bill/coin	billet/monnaie

HEALTH

doctor/dentist/	médecin/dentiste/
paediatrician	pédiatre
hospital/emergency clinic	hôpital/urgences
fever/pain	fièvre/douleurs
diarrhoea/nausea	diarrhée/nausée
sunburn	coup de soleil
inflamed/injured	enflammé/blessé
plaster/bandage	pansement/bandage
ointment/pain reliever	pommade/analgésique

POST, TELECOMMUNICATIONS & MEDIA

stamp	timbre
letter/postcard	lettre/carte postale
I need a landline phone card	J'ai besoin d'une carte téléphonique pour fixe.
I'm looking for a prepaid card for my mobile	Je cherche une recharge pour mon portable.
Where can I find internet access?	Où puis-je trouver un accès à internet?
dial/connection/engaged	composer/connection/occupé
socket/charger	prise électrique/chargeur
computer/battery/rechargeable battery	ordinateur/batterie/accumulateur
at sign (@)	arobase
internet address (URL)/e-mail address	adresse internet/mail
internet connection/wi-fi	accès internet/wi-fi
e-mail/file/print	mail/fichier/imprimer

LEISURE, SPORTS & BEACH

beach	plage
sunshade/lounger	parasol/transat
low tide/high tide/current	marée basse/marée haute/courant
cable car/chair lift	téléphérique/télésiège
(rescue) hut	refuge

NUMBERS

0	zéro	17	dix-sept
1	un, une	18	dix-huite
2	deux	19	dix-neuf
3	trois	20	vingt
4	quatre	30	trente
5	cinq	40	quarante
6	six	50	cinquante
7	sept	60	soixante
8	huit	70	soixante-dix
9	neuf	80	quatre-vingt
10	dix	90	quatre-vingt-dix
11	onze	100	cent
12	douze	200	deux cents
13	treize	1,000	mille
14	quatorze		
15	quinze	½	un[e] demi[e]
16	seize	¼	un quart

ROAD ATLAS

The green line indicates the Discovery Tour "The Seychelles at a glance"
The blue line indicates the other Discovery Tours

All tours are also marked on the pull-out map

Photo: Anse Intendance, Mahé

Exploring the Seychelles

The map on the back cover shows how the area has been sub-divided

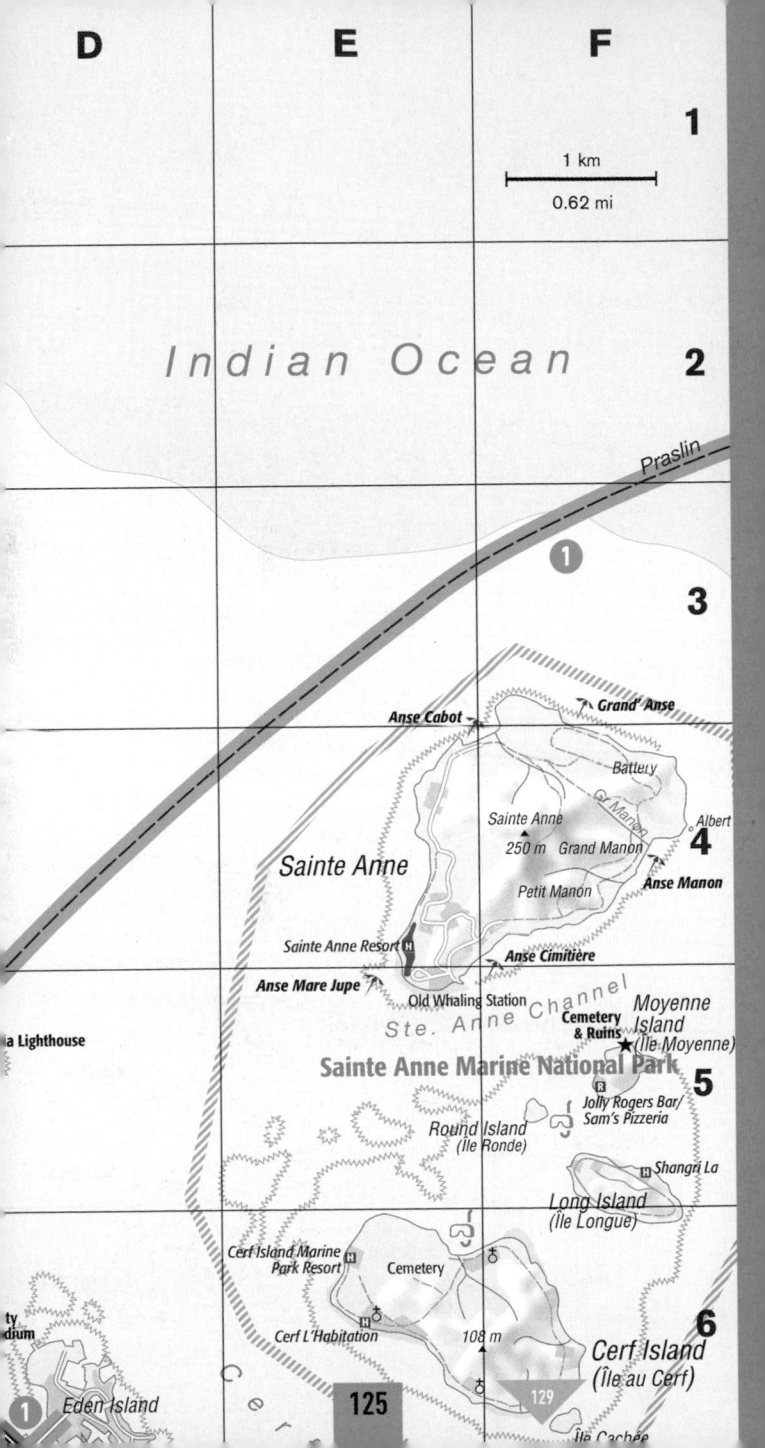

D　　　E　　　F

1

1 km
0.62 mi

I n d i a n   O c e a n

2

Praslin

①

3

Anse Cabot ↗ Grand' Anse

Battery

Sainte Anne ▲
250 m Grand Manon

Sainte Anne

Petit Manon

Albert ○

Anse Manon **4**

Sainte Anne Resort Ⓗ

Anse Mare Jupe ↗

Old Whaling Station

Anse Cimitière

Ste. Anne Channel

Moyenne
Island
(Île Moyenne)

a Lighthouse

Cemetery
& Ruins ★

Sainte Anne Marine National Park

Ⓡ Jolly Rogers Bar/
Sam's Pizzeria

5

Round Island
(Île Ronde)

Ⓗ Shangri La

Long Island
(Île Longue)

Cerf Island Marine Ⓗ
Park Resort

Cemetery

ty
drum

Cerf L'Habitation

108 m ▲

Cerf

Cerf Island
(Île au Cerf)

6

① Eden Island

125

129 ▽

Île Cachée

A　　　**B**　　　**C**

1

2

3

4

5

6

Danzil

Poulalier
▲ *206 m*

Anse Major Nature Trail

Jasmin

Anse Major
(Anse Jasmin)

Anse Jasmin Estate

Major

Moustache

Baie aux Chagrins

Cap Ternay

C a p T e r n a y E s t a t e

Baie Ternay

Du Riz

Mte

Anse du Riz

Morne Seychellois National Park

Baie Ternay
Marine National Park

Pointe
Matoopa

C a p M a t o o p a

Souillac

**Anse
Souillac**

Port Launay

L e   P a s s e   T e r n a y

Port Launay
Marine National Park

Port Launay

La Pl

Anse des Anglais

Pointe L'Escalier ★

Ephelia Re

L'Embarcadère

Conception

Theresa Ⓡ

Thérèse
▲ *160 m*

Thérèse Island

I n d i a n   O c e a n

D   *Île Cachée*   **E**   **F**

1

1 km
0.62 mi

a s s a g e

Mahé

2

ris

Île Anonyme
37 m
Île Anonyme

Providence Highway

②
Cascade
Cap Ma Georgine

Île aux Rats

er Wheel ★ ♦ St. André

Anse Talbot

Passenger
Terminal ✈ **Seychelles**
International Airport

Île du Suète

Cascade

Talbot ✿

Cargo Terminal
Aero Club

Helistop

3

Anse Déjeuner

Mont Sebert   **Pointe Larue**

François

Les Dents
555 m

Pointe La Rue

②

Anse Faure

Varigault

Mondon

Ⓗ *Carefree Guesthous* **4**

Grand Bassin

Capucins

Anse aux Pins

Ⓗ
✿ *La Retraite*

Longue Mare

s

⟋ Anse aux Pins

5

oir *Bon Espoir*

La Réserve

Nageon

Ⓗ *Casuarina Beach*

St. Joseph

Chemin Montagne Posée

Creole Institute
(Maison St. Joseph) ★

Brulée Nature Trail

★ **Roche Amour** *Du Cap*

St. Roch Estate

le & Wireless
llite Tracking
Station

Le Domaine de Val des Près ★
Vilaz Artizanal

②

Le Cap

Mte. Brulée
501 m

Piton de L'Eboulis

La Plaine St. Andre

6

Ecomuseum Ⓜ

La Marine ★
Model Ships

⟋ Anse aux Courbes

Anse Louis

129

131

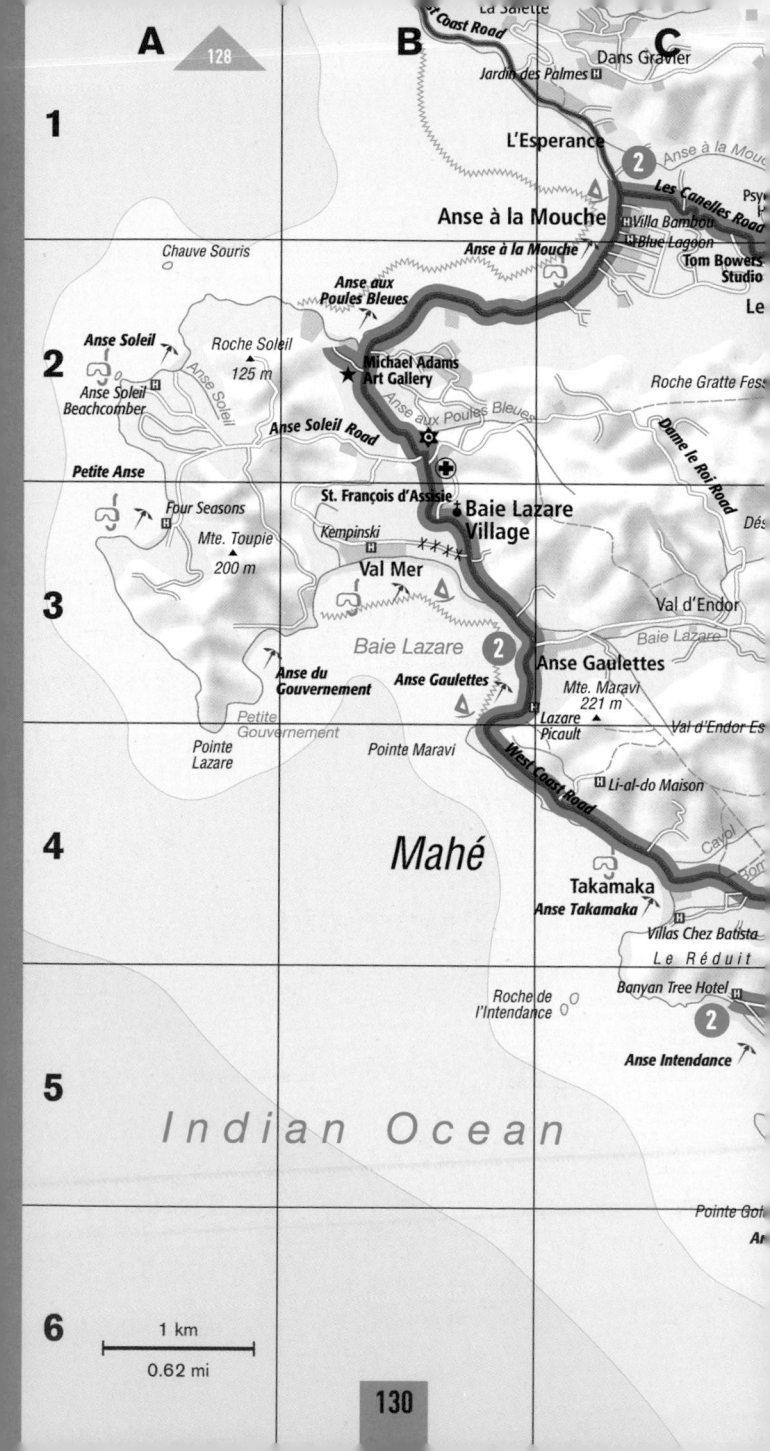

La Salette

st Coast Road

Jardin des Palmes H

Dans Gravier

1

L'Esperance

Anse à la Mouche

2

Les Canelles Road

Psy

Anse à la Mouche

H Villa Bambou

H Blue Lagoon

Tom Bowers
Studio

Le

Chauve Souris

Anse aux
Poules Bleues

Roche Gratte Fess

Anse Soleil

Roche Soleil

2

125 m

Michael Adams
★ Art Gallery

Anse Soleil
Beachcomber

Anse Soleil Road

Dame le Roi Road

Petite Anse

St. François d'Assisie

✝ Baie Lazare
Village

Dés

Four Seasons

H Mte. Toupie

Kempinski

Val Mer

221 m

Val d'Endor

3

Baie Lazare

2

Val d'Endor

Anse Gaulettes

Anse du
Gouvernement

Anse Gaulettes

Mte. Maravi
221 m

Val d'Endor Es

Petite
Gouvernement

Lazare
Picault

Pointe
Lazare

Pointe Maravi

West Coast Road

H Li-al-do Maison

4

Mahé

Takamaka

Anse Takamaka

H Villas Chez Batista

Le Réduit

Roche de
l'Intendance

Banyan Tree Hotel H

2

Anse Intendance

5

Indian Ocean

Pointe Go

Ar

6

1 km

0.62 mi

D   **E**   **F**

nt Plaisir

Moripa

T. Butler

2

129

1

*Piton Jean Marie
(Oliver Hill)
232 m*

Pointe au Sel

Monte Cristo

St. Antoine   *Le Relax*

Fairyland

Pointe au Sel

Souris

Kaz Kreol

Anse Royale

2

Royale

Sweet Escott Road

2

Anse Royale

ncement

Le Jardin du Roi ★

*Anse Royale
Bay*

Désert

30 m

Terrain Maillet

Anse Baleine

3

Bougainville

Anse Bougainville

d'Endor Road

Bougainville

Anse Parnel

2

*Mont Parnel
378*

Cap Lascar

*Cap Lascars
(Cap Maçons)*

4

Clovis

South Coast Rd.

Anse Forbans

Chalets d'Anse Forbans

Anse Forbans

Anse Marie Louise

atre Bornes

Anse Marie Louise

ntendance

Quatre Bornes

Petite Marie Louise

5

*Beau Séjour
301 m
Mont Cauvin*

Robert

Collines du Sud

*tagne
chée*

*Mte.
Corail*

*Pointe
Capucins*

Anse Capucins

Grande Police Road

Giraffe

*Pointe
Cocos*

Grande Police

Montagne Capucines

6

e Corail

Anse Bazarca

Petite Police

Petite Boileau

*Pointe du Sud
(Cap Malheureux)*

Police Bay

131

Police Point

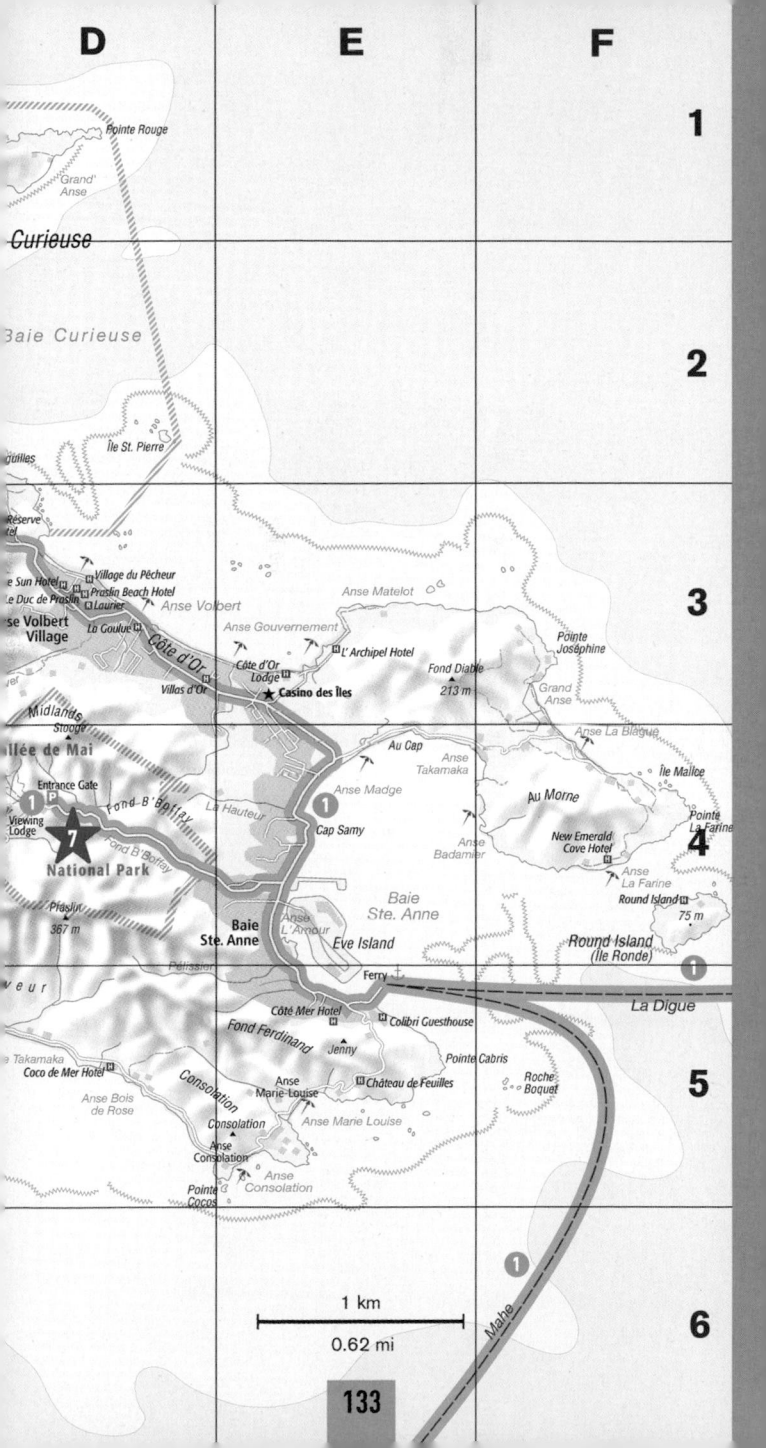

D   E   F

1

Pointe Rouge

Grand' Anse

Curieuse

Baie Curieuse

2

Île St. Pierre

iguilles

éserve
tel

3

e Sun Hotel   Village du Pêcheur
Duc de Praslin   Praslin Beach Hotel
    Laurier

Anse Volbert

Anse Matelot

e Volbert
Village

La Goulue

Anse Gouvernement

Côte d'Or

L' Archipel Hotel   Pointe
    Joséphine

Côte d'Or
Lodge

Fond Diable
213 m

Grand
Anse

Villas d'Or

★ Casino des Îles

Midlands
   Stooge

Anse La Blague

e de Mai

4

❶ Entrance Gate

Au Cap

Anse
Takamaka

Île Mallce

Fond B' Boffay

La Hauteur

Anse Madge

Au Morne

Viewing
Lodge

❶

Fond B' Boffay

Cap Samy

Anse
Badamier

New Emerald
Cove Hotel

Pointe
La Farine

7

National Park

Baie
Ste. Anne

Anse
La Farine

Praslin
367 m

**Baie
STE. ANNE**

Anse
L'Amour

Round Island
    75 m

Eve Island

Round Island
(Île Ronde)

Palissaie

❶

e u r

Ferry ⚓

La Digue

5

Côté Mer Hotel

Colibri Guesthouse

e Takamaka
Coco de Mer Hotel

Fond Ferdinand

Jenny

Pointe Cabris

Château de Feuilles

Roche
Boquet

Consolation

Anse
Marie-Louise

Anse Bois
de Rose

Consolation

Anse Marie Louise

Anse
Consolation

Pointe
Cocos

Anse
Consolation

6

❶

1 km

0.62 mi

Mahé

133

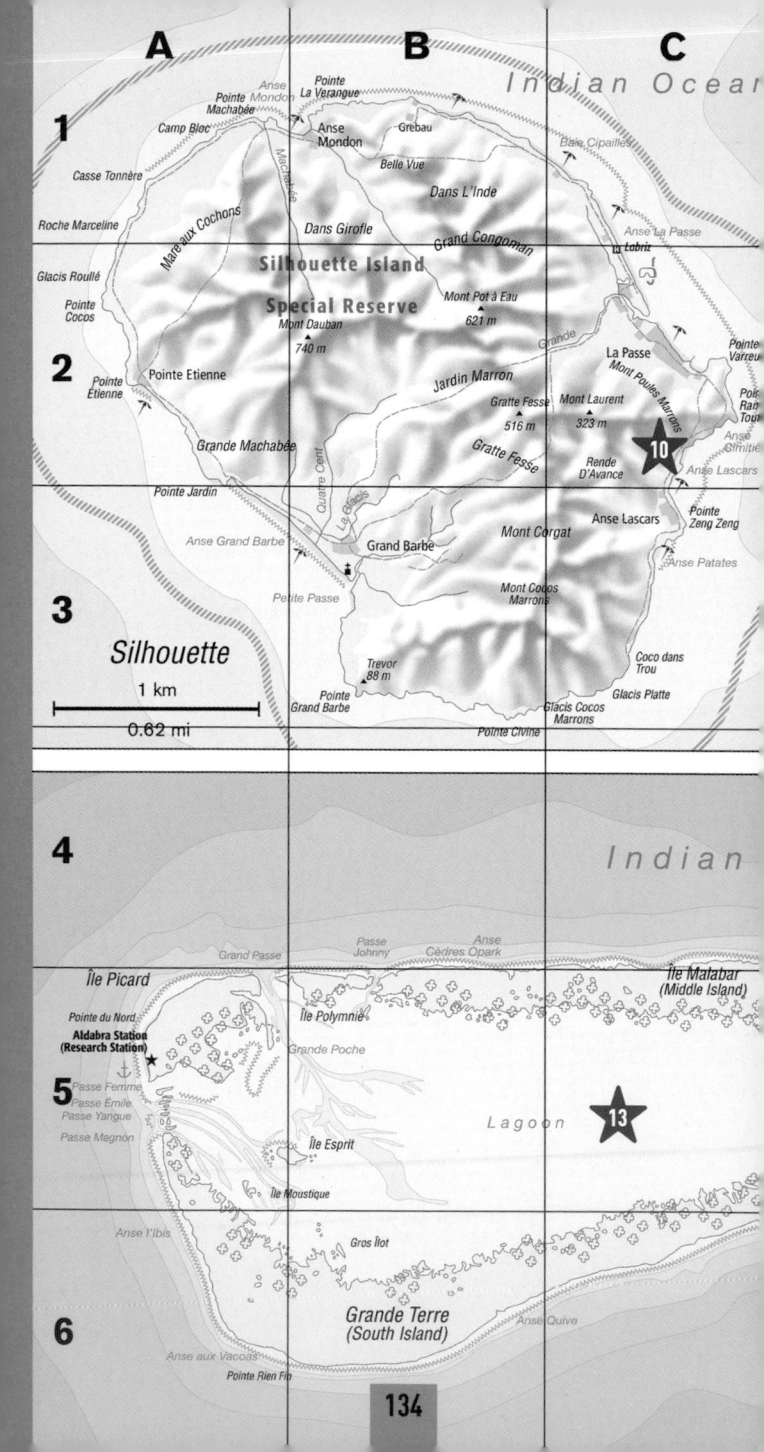

A

B

C

1

Indian Ocean

Pointe Mondon
Anse Machabée
Pointe La Verangue
Camp Bloc
Anse Mondon
Grebau
Belle Vue
Baie Cipailles
Casse Tonnère
Dans L'Inde
Roche Marceline
Dans Girofle
Grand Congoman
Anse La Passe
Labrit

Glacis Roullé
Silhouette Island
Mare aux Cochons
Special Reserve
Pointe Cocos
Mont Pot à Eau
621 m
Grande
Pointe Varreu

2

Pointe Etienne
Mont Dauban
740 m
La Passe
Mont Poules Marrons
Pointe Etienne
Jardin Marron
Mont Laurent
323 m
Poir Ram Tour
Gratte Fesse
516 m
Anse Clmitie
Grande Machabée
Gratte Fesse
Rende D'Avance
10
Anse Lascars

3

Pointe Jardin
Anse Lascars
Pointe Zeng Zeng
Anse Grand Barbe
Mont Corgat
Le Glacis
Quatre Cent
Grand Barbe
Anse Patates

Silhouette

Petite Passe
Mont Cocos Marrons

1 km

0.62 mi

Trevor
88 m
Coco dans Trou
Pointe Grand Barbe
Glacis Cocos Marrons
Glacis Platte
Pointe Civine

4

Indian

5

Grand Passe
Passe Johnny
Anse Cèdres Opark
Île Picard
Île Malabar
(Middle Island)
Pointe du Nord
**Aldabra Station
(Research Station)** ★
Île Polymnie
Passe Femme
Grande Poche
Passe Emile
Passe Yangue
Lagoon
13
Passe Magnon
Île Esprit
Île Moustique

6

Anse l'Ibis
Gros Îlot
Grande Terre
(South Island)
Anse Quive
Anse aux Vacoas
Pointe Rien Fin

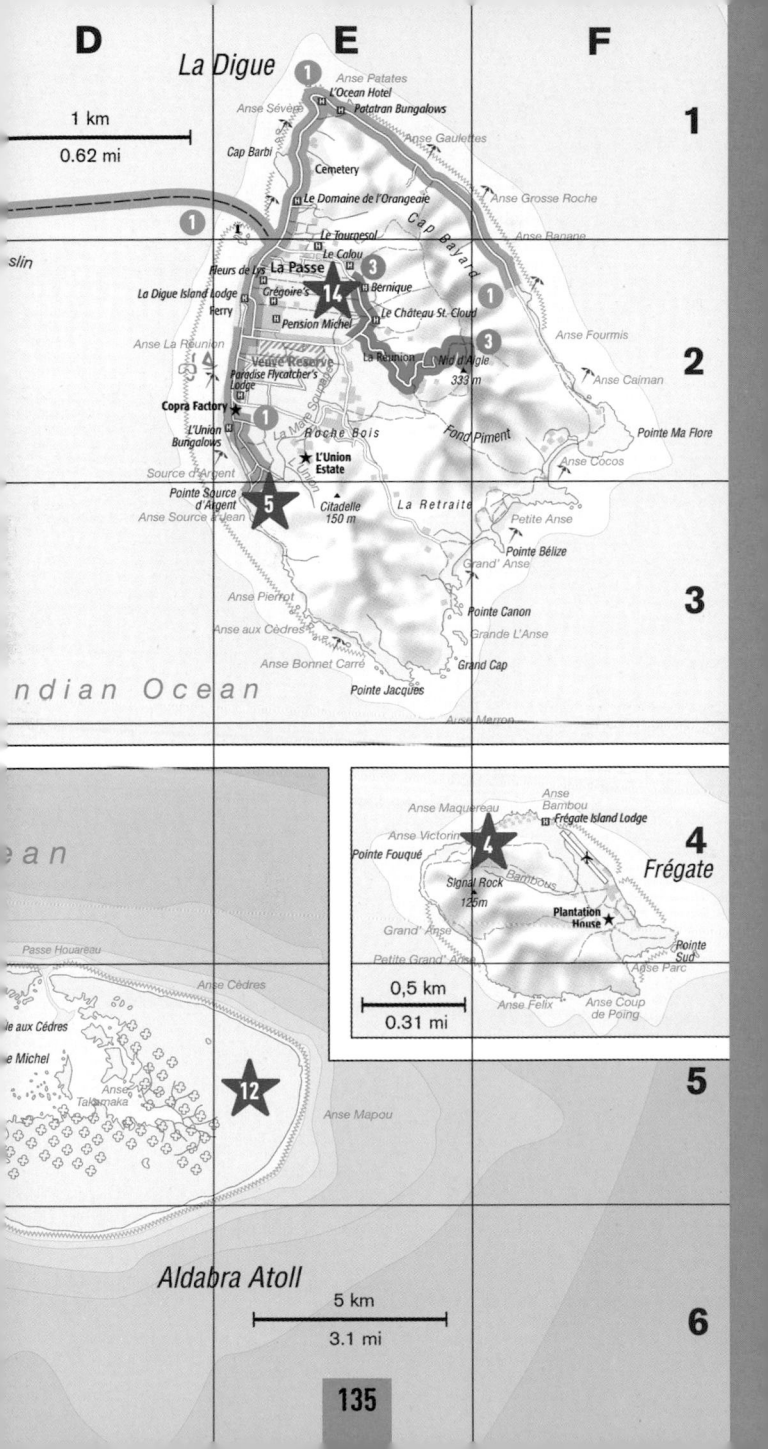

La Digue

1 km
0.62 mi

D · **E** · **F**

1

Anse Patates
L'Ocean Hotel
Anse Sévère · Patatran Bungalows
Anse Gaulettes
Cap Barbi
Cemetery · Anse Grosse Roche
Le Domaine de l'Orangeaie
Cap Bayard · Anse Banane
Le Tournesol
Le Calou
Fleurs de Lys · La Passe · **3**
La Digue Island Lodge · Crégoire's · Le Bernique · **1**
Ferry · Pension Michel · Le Château St. Cloud
Anse Fourmis
Anse La Réunion · **3**
Veuve Reserve · La Réunion · Nid d'Aigle
Paradise Flycatcher's · La Meze Street · 333 m · Anse Caiman
Lodge
Copra Factory · **1**
L'Union · Roche Bois · Fond Piment · Pointe Ma Flore
Bungalows · Anse Cocos
Source d'Argent · L'Union · Estate
Pointe Source · **5** · Citadelle · La Retraite
d'Argent · 150 m · Petite Anse
Anse Source d'Jean · Pointe Bélize
Anse Pierrot · Grand' Anse
Anse aux Cèdres · Pointe Canon · Grande L'Anse
Anse Bonnet Carré · Grand Cap
ndian Ocean · Pointe Jacques
Anse Merron

2

3

---

4 · Frégate

Anse Maquereau · Anse Bambou
Anse Victorin · Frégate Island Lodge
Pointe Fouqué · **4**
Signal Rock · Bambous
125m · Plantation House
Grand' Anse · Pointe Sud
Petite Grand' Anse · Anse Parc
Anse Coup
Anse Felix · de Poing

0,5 km
0.31 mi

5

ean

Passe Houareau
Anse Cèdres
le aux Cèdres · Anse Cèdres
e Michel · Anse Mapou
Anse Takamaka · **12**

Aldabra Atoll

5 km
3.1 mi

6

KEY TO ROAD ATLAS

Fernstraße Highway	
Hauptstraße Main road	
Nebenstraßen Secondary road	
Fahrweg Carriage way	
Fußweg Pedestrian way	
Riff Reef	
Nationalpark, Naturreservat National Park, nature reserve	
Mariner Nationalpark Marine National Park	
Aussichtspunkt Panoramic view	
Mangroven Mangroves	
Windsurfing Windsurfing	
Schnorcheln Snorkeling	
Tauchen Diving	
Parkplatz Parking	

H R Hotel; Restaurant
Hotel; restaurant

Kirche
Church

Krankenhaus
Hospital

Polizei
Police

M Museum
Museum

Leuchtturm
Lighthouse

★ Sehenswürdigkeit
Point of interest

Botanischer Garten
Botanical garden

Tankstelle
Gas station

▲ · Berggipfel; Höhenpunkt
Mountain top; geodetic point

Badestrand
Beach

Internationaler Flughafen
International airport

Flughafen
Airport

Flugplatz
Aerodrome

MARCO POLO Erlebnistour 1
MARCO POLO Discovery Tour 1

MARCO POLO Erlebnistouren
MARCO POLO Discovery Tours

★1 MARCO POLO Highlight

FOR YOUR NEXT TRIP...

MARCO POLO TRAVEL GUIDES

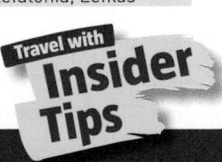

Travel with
Insider
Tips

INDEX

This index lists all islands, towns and bays as well as names and key words featured in this guide. Numbers in bold indicate a main entry.

WRITE TO US

e-mail: sales@heartwoodpublishing.co.uk

Did you have a great holiday?
Is there something on your mind?
Whatever it is, let us know! Whether you
want to praise, alert us to errors or give us
a personal tip – MARCO POLO would be
pleased to hear from you.

We do everything we can to provide the
very latest information for your
trip.Nevertheless, despite all of our
authors' thorough research, errors can
creep in. MARCO POLO does not accept any
ability for this. Please contact us by e-mail.

PICTURE CREDITS
Cover photograph: Granite boulder at Anse Source d'Argent beach (Look: T. Grundner)
Photos: Tom Bowers (18 centre); DuMont Bildarchiv: Huber (40, 111); Holger Ehlert (18 bottom); Getty Images: Ghislain & Marie David de Lossy (2), S. Layda (26/27); Getty Images/AWL Images RM (12/13); Getty Images/Image Source (3); Glowimages: T. Haltner (4 top, glowimages: T. Haltner (74/75); H. Gstaltmayr (6, 39); Huber-images: C. Dörr (17); huber-images: Mehlig (32/33), Ripani (62), Schmid (flap right, 28 left, 44); Huber-images: R. Schmid (47, 52/53, 96/97, 122/123); ©iStockphoto: Ian McDonnell (19 top); KREOLOR LTD: Gilbert Pool (18 top); La Terra Magica: Lenz (flap left, 110 bottom); laif: Kirchgessner (28 right), T. Linkel (61, 79); Laif: Martin (99); laif: M. Vogel (9); laif/Fautre/Le Figaro Magazine (73); laif/hemis.fr: Degas (20/21); laif/Le Figaro Magazine: Fautre (82); Look: T. Grundner (1 top); Look/age fotostock (109); Look/age-foto (10); Look/NordicPhotos (107); LOOK-foto: J. Greune (43); LOOK-foto/age-foto (67); mauritius images: W. Bibikow (65), M. Runkel (106); mauritius images/age-foto: L. Davilla (70); mauritius images/Alamy (4 bottom, Afripics (68/69), Couloria Media (51), Danita Delmont Creative (54), M. Falzone (93), E. Gerald (108), N. Macutti (30/31); mauritius images/Alamy/STOCKFOLIO® (101); mauritius images/CuboImages: M. Casiraghi (58); mauritius images/imageBROKER: Andrey Nekrasov (76), W. Lang (34, 95), M. Moxter (8, 31); mauritius images/Westend61/WeEmm (56); H. Mielke (5, 7, 11, 14/15, 30 left, 48, 80/81, 85, 87, 102/103, 104, 110 top); Schapowalow: F. Carassale/SIME (37), Fabrizio Romiti/SIME (108/109), M. Ripani/SIME (29), R. Schmid (25, 88/89); P. Spierenburg (22); Wilderness Safaris: Dana Allen (19 bottom)

2nd edition– fully revised and updated 2020
Worldwide Distribution: Marco Polo Travel Publishing Ltd, Pinewood, Chineham
Business Park, Crockford Lane, Basingstoke, Hampshire RG24 8AL, United Kingdom. Email: sales@marcopolouk.com
© MAIRDUMONT GmbH & Co. KG, Ostfildern
Chief editor: Stefanie Penck
Author: Heiner F. Gstaltmayr, co-author: Heike Mallad; editor: Jochen Schürmann
Programme supervision: Susanne Heimburger, Tamara Hub, Nikolai Michaelis, Kristin Schimpf, Martin Silbermann
Picture editors: Gabriele Forst, Barbara Mehrl; What's hot: wunder media, Munich; cartography road atlas:
DuMont Reisekartografie, Fürstenfeldbruck; © MAIRDUMONT, Ostfildern; cartography pull-out map: DuMont
Reisekartografie, Fürstenfeldbruck; © MAIRDUMONT, Ostfildern
Cover design, p. 1, pull-out map cover: Karl Anders – Büro für Visual Stories, Hamburg; Gestaltung
Design inside: milchhof:atelier, Berlin; design p. 2/3, Discovery Tours: Susan Chaaban Dipl.-Des. (FH)
Translated from German by Nicole Meyer and Dr. Suzanne Kirkbright
Editorial office: SAW Communications, Redaktionsbüro Dr. Sabine A. Werner, Mainz: Julia Gilcher, Sariya Sloan,
Cosima Talhouni, Dr. Sabine A. Werner; prepress: SAW Communications, Mainz, in cooperation with alles mit
Medien, Mainz
Phrase book in cooperation with Ernst Klett Sprachen GmbH, Stuttgart,
Editorial by Pons Wörterbücher

MIX
Paper from
responsible sources
FSC® C016779
www.fsc.org

DOS & DON'TS ✋

A few things to look out for on your Seychelles holiday

DO DRIVE WITH CAUTION

Mahé, the main island, is fun to discover by car but a word of caution: driving under the influence of alcohol can quickly turn your adventure into a dangerous outing. Many roads lack guard rails and shoulders and have steep drops instead. In addition many locals have a driving style that affords little consideration to the visitor.

DO OBEY NATURE CONSERVATION RULES

It is a given that you always take your rubbish with you when leaving the beach and obey the 'No Smoking' signs – such as in the Vallée de Mai on Praslin. Smoking poses a real danger, especially in the dry months. Hiking trails are sign-posted, so keep to the path to avoid trampling on protected plants. And a request to divers and snorkellers: marine creatures, especially corals, should remain where they are.

DO AVOID SOUVENIRS MADE FROM TORTOISESHELL

Once you have seen how the shell is removed from a tortoise, you would voluntarily forego buying souvenirs made of tortoise shell. Unfortunately these products, which are banned in the Seychelles, are still sold in some shops. Besides, importing products that derive from protected animals or plants is a punishable offense in EU countries and the USA.

DON'T GIVE THIEVES AN OPPORTUNITY

In recent years minor thefts and scams have increased on a small scale and there are even reports of cars being broken into. It is therefore best that you don't carry more money than is necessary and never leave valuables – mobile phones and cameras – in the car. And never display a bulging wallet...

DON'T IGNORE SWIMMING SIGNS

Red danger signs on the beaches indicate that swimming is not allowed or warn of dangerous currents and these signs should never be ignored. These signs are there with good reason as these currents regularly claim lives.

DON'T DISTURB RELIGIOUS EVENTS

Imagine a group of tourists barging into a service at your church and taking pictures while you are saying the Lord's Prayer! It should be a given that you do not to disturb religious gatherings in this way. And yet there are still people that find a church with believers more photogenic than one without. Taking pictures in front of the church is not a problem, the Seychellios are usually happy to oblige.